IT   HAPPENED
HERE

An Impression of part of the Fifty-horse cavalcade taking the King of Denmark over the pennine moorland road after leaving Halifax in 1768 (see "A King came for a night").

It Happened Here

EVENTS AND INCIDENTS THAT HAVE ENLIVENED, DISTURBED, OR ADDED INTEREST TO THE LIVES OF THE PEOPLE IN TOWN, VILLAGE AND COUNTRY IN A WIDE AREA CENTRING UPON HALIFAX DURING THE PAST THREE CENTURIES. RECALLED FROM RECORDS AND REWRITTEN BY

ARTHUR PORRITT

E. J. MORTEN (Publishers)
Didsbury, Manchester, England

First Printed 1955
FAWCETT, GREENWOOD & CO. LTD.
Well Lane, Halifax

ISBN 0 901598 40 2

© A. PORRITT 1955

Republished 1972
E. J. MORTEN (Publishers)/E & L Ass.
10 Warburton Street, Didsbury,
Manchester, England

Printed in Great Britain by
Scolar Press Limited, Menston, Yorkshire

INTRODUCTION

These stories of happenings during the past three centuries were selected from a series that appeared in the *Halifax Courier & Guardian* weekly issues from November 1952 to February 1959, under the title 'It Happened Here'. In view of popular demand they were printed in this easy-to-read form in this First Series book in 1955, and were continued in the Second and Third Series books in 1959 and 1969 under the same title. The two earlier volumes having been long out of print and thus unobtainable, the present reprint has been felt justified by continued demand; and for republication of this First Series book I am indebted to the Publishers whose imprint it bears.

It is not possible to name the innumerable authorities, historians, reporters, authors of articles, notes and paragraphs in countless early copies of local and other newspapers and of matter consulted: many of them, indeed, have long since departed. To all, however, and especially to the management and staff of the newspaper mentioned for their interest and encouragement and to the libraries staffs who made possible the research involved in recalling the long past and, in many cases, almost forgotten incidents and events, my appreciation is extended; and to all interested in past happenings in the part of Yorkshire centring around Halifax the series is dedicated.

Halifax, 1972.   A. PORRITT

The Opening of Halifax Zoo.

" HALIFAX ZOO! Most up-to-date amusement park in England! Great attraction for Whit Monday and Tuesday! Admission 6d." This announcement on May 29, 1909, and much early publicity, attracted 41,000 people to Chevinedge that Whit week-end.

Many surprises awaited them. Extensive grounds, the amusement park promised by the advertisements, a lake still under construction and —greatest attraction—the new zoo. The enterprise was not completed for the opening day, but this did not lessen the enthusiasm displayed by people from many miles around.

An elephant had accompanied the King Cross Band on parades in the streets. A sensation was caused when this elephant took fright at a tram and bolted near the bottom of Salterhebble, scaring the crowds that had been attracted, and finally stumbling and falling over. The animal recovered itself without injury.

With a white Arabian camel this 17-year-old elephant had walked from Halifax on arrival. Three truck-loads of smaller animals had been delivered three weeks previously; and these, with the sight from time to time of strange vehicles bringing stranger animals and birds through the town whetted the anticipation of the people.

There was no formal opening : the gates were simply thrown back for the crowds to pay their sixpences and enter—having mostly ascended Exley Bank from the relays of special trams that Halifax had provided. The zoo was well stocked, and up to the opening day the aviaries were being filled with specimens of gaily plumaged birds from South America and Australia, with an eagle and a vulture in their special cage. An Indian calf, born in the zoo the day before the opening, was on view. Two African lions, two bears, hyenas, jackals, wolves, zebras, a yak— all were there to greet the flocking crowds. The monkey-house was a prominent attraction. A white dromedary from Egypt was still to come, as partner for the Arabian camel.

A pigmy farm was a novel feature. Here one stepped over a stile and along a path leading to a tiny farmhouse fitted ready for a dwarf man and wife who were to occupy it. There were a model stable, pigsty and mistal, and pigmy animals moved about the farm. A full-grown sheep there weighed only eight pounds.

The lake was to have a section for the display of tropical plants : it was to have its black and white swans, and ducks from China and India, and a fountain playing. Music was provided by local and other bands from an ornamental bandstand while a refreshment conservatory was a popular rendezvous. This opening night was enlivened by a grand firework display and a variety entertainment.

1

When the Bear got away from Halifax Zoo

WHEN the bear escaped from the Zoo at Chevinedge, on June 17, 1913, the news spread like wildfire. There was great excitement in Siddal when it was learned that the bear was heading in that direction and had actually got into Jubilee Road. A number of people made themselves secure in their homes, but many curious residents collected warily. Actually two bears had escaped from their cages near the zoo entrance, but one of them had been captured and secured by keepers before he could leave the grounds. The other had gained his freedom while the keepers were thus occupied, and he went off at a loping run down Exley Bank. From here he had turned into Jubilee Road.

He was left a clear run as people scattered out of his way, but the head keeper, Mr. Hinds, contrived to get ahead of him and to turn him back. The bear eluded him by jumping a wall into a field and making off towards Backhold Hill, but he turned down eventually into Elland Wood.

In hot pursuit, Mr. Hinds and other helpers finally got to close quarters, but recapture among the trees on the steeply sloping ground proved difficult and dangerous. It was impossible to lasso the animal; at one stage the keeper drove him into a corner and with conspicuous pluck tried to put a rope round his head. In this he was unsuccessful, as the bear was too quick for him; and Mr. Hinds then found himself in a close-up tussle with the beast, his coat, waistcoat and trousers being torn in the encounter. Fortunately a rope slipped round the bear's legs secured the animal after a further struggle, for he was by this time roused to fury and was most probably frightened by the excitement after his long enforced captivity. He had been at liberty—if this sort of freedom could be called liberty—for two hours.

But capture was not the end. It proved a formidable task to get the angry bear back to the zoo. He refused to walk more than two hundred yards along Elland Wood Bottom, and he had to be held there until a dray carrying a cage was brought down. In this he was returned up Exley Bank to the safety of his quarters.

The bears proved a popular exhibit after this escapade, but the time soon came for them to disappear with all the other occupants. The zoo closed down and its stock was dispersed to various other provincial zoos, in this fifth year of its existence here.

The Pye Nest Tram Disaster.

IT is not easy to realise that little more than half a century ago electric tramcars had not begun running in Halifax streets (although the town was one of the earliest in the north to introduce them) and that it is already fourteen years since our last tram made its farewell journey. For nearly forty-one years they served the town and the outlying districts, carrying many millions of passengers. The happiest event must surely have been the day in 1898 when thousands of people assembled to see the official opening of the service, as three new cars, gaily decorated and carrying Corporation officials, set out on their first journey. Some difficulty was experienced by these trams in negotiating the curves in Silver Street, but once on the straight in King Cross Lane everything went well, and they had a tremendous welcome from the watching crowds.

It was not long before the rails reached out to Sowerby Bridge, and on this route the most tragic happening in the history of our electric tramways occurred, only nine years after their inauguration. A car left Sowerby Bridge for Halifax at 5-40 one morning, both decks packed with passengers going to work. It had ascended the hill as far as the Pye Nest bend, when, without warning, it came to a stop and began to run back. The driver could do nothing to check its downward rush and the conductor, who was on the open upper deck collecting fares, was equally powerless when he ran down to his platform. He found a passenger trying to apply the brake, but all efforts were useless. The swinging trolley pole was wrenched from its support on the tram top by one of the cross wires from a standard, and it hung dangerously loose as the car rapidly gained speed down the long gradient.

The tram kept to the rails the whole distance down to Bolton Brow, but at the slight bend it left them and crashed into a shop front, swinging completely round before overturning. The upper deck had been forced off by the impact and fell in the roadway where school-children would have been crowding a little later.

It was stated at the inquiry that the tram was fitted with an automatic " run-back " brake, but it was ineffective in this emergency. Five people were killed, including the conductor, and more than forty were injured. A memorial stone for which subscriptions were raised, stands over the grave of the conductor in Mount Zion Chapel burial ground at Ogden, the inscription recording his bravery.

Balloon Ascent from Crow Wood Park

THE big balloon was 6,000 feet up—quite a height for people to be over the district half a century ago. It was watched by thousands as it passed over forty miles of country and town until it could no longer be seen in the darkness. Other balloons were in the local air that day in 1906, for Sowerby Bridge had launched them during the gala in Crow Wood Park to celebrate fifty years of the town's local government. But the huge captive balloon, the " Prince of Wales," had drawn the crowds as it was filled with gas (from the mains) and again when Mr. Bramhall, of Bradford, and his assistant Mr. Wood took their places in the passenger cabin and left the park for the sky.

They had a wonderful journey, which they covered at thirty miles an hour. Mr. Bramhall reported having passed over Halifax, Salter-hebble, Brighouse, Bradford, Wakefield and other places, the lights of Leeds and the glowing furnaces of Sheffield being impressive distant sights from their lofty view point. Earlier in their flight as they came down intending to land they had to let out ballast because they could not find suitable landing ground. They rose again to full height, finally coming to earth near Doncaster, and they recorded that they had descended from six thousand feet in five minutes.

During the same year the first parachute descent made in this district by a woman was an advertised event at a gala held at Haworth. The parachutist, 21 years old, who was touring the country demonstrating jumps from a balloon, had previously made twenty successful descents—but this one had a tragic ending. The wind carried the balloon towards the moors near Stanbury. There the girl leaped from the swaying pannier, but her parachute failed to open and the thousands of horrified spectators saw only the girl's body hurtling to the ground, near Ponden Reservoir. At the inquest the jury recommended that such performances as dropping by parachute should be prohibited by Act of Parliament.

Only four years later Mr. Grahame White made his locally famous flights in his biplane, the first aeroplane flights in Halifax. He took off from the West End Golf Club links for his five demonstration flights, the longest lasting about thirteen minutes, and circled over the zoo at Exley in his circuits of the town. He attained a height of 1,000 feet on this occasion—which was little more than six years after the first flight by a heavier-than-air machine.

The Salt Pie auction.

HUNDREDS of people climbed a Luddenden hillside one morning in 1905 to a little whitewashed cottage where Thomas Longbottom —" Tommy o' t' Salt Pie "—had died aged 77. The contents of his two-roomed home were being sold. During the 50 years he had worked at the paper mills at Booth he had devoted his spare moments to collecting " odd " things, and had assembled a medley that filled the cottage and the two sheds he built to house his expanding museum. Tommy could not write; but he could read the advertisements in the " Halifax Courier " and the " Exchange & Mart " and could get replies written for him.

The Halifax auctioneer, Mr. Harrison, had nearly 1,000 articles to dispose of, and a hot day on which to sell them to a crowd of good-natured picnickers. So hot was it that some people fainted. It was the sort of sale at which an enterprising vendor of meat pies provided distracting competition. On the low sloping roof of the cottage the smaller articles were piled, the rest being amassed outside. Ornaments, utensils, tea-pots—one of three gallons, another of two gallons capacity, with monster cups in support; a Russian coffin, for which bids rose from sixpence to 1s. 2d. when the auctioneer opened it " to see who was inside," and revealed a doll. Tommy's two live parrots, and a pair of stuffed pigeons bearing an announcement that they, too, had lived with Tommy " to the great age of 31 years " sold for 4s. 6d. with a stuffed canary. A model of Mr. Gladstone felling a tree sold with a stuffed monkey for 1s. d., and a bust of Queen Victoria with some stuffed animals for two pence. But £2 10s. in gold was paid for a cage marked " Made in Germany " containing two birds which sang when Mr. Harrison dropped a penny in the slot. The purchaser of this lot found its value was almost doubled by the contents!

A street organ, hurdy-gurdies and musical boxes in the collection all had to be played before being knocked down, so the sale became at times a concert of old-time popular airs. These instruments, like the many ingenious working models of figures that were Tommy's speciality, were in good working order. So were his 63 clocks. There were curious walking-sticks, and—selling privately for 35s.—there was a 33-hundred-weight block of coal that he had built into one of the sheds 24 years earlier. This sale of Tommy's life-time acquisitions realised under £60 for his widow.

To Well Head for Kew.

IF you felt like seeing the summer display at Kew Gardens fifty years ago but had to deny yourself this delight, you could have seen them in miniature without leaving Halifax. You need only have asked permission from Mrs. Doherty Waterhouse to look round her gardens at Well Head, which had been in existence since about 1800. They contained plants, ferns, trees, cacti and rare specimens of horticulture collected by the Waterhouse family from all parts of the world. There were several greenhouses, and the head gardener and his five under-gardeners knew how to display the contents to their best advantage.

A fountain played in the centre of the camellia house, where camellias were planted out in beds, while round the stages were orange trees in pots, cacti and hardy ferns. There were plants brought from the banks of the Amazon, ferns from Australia, a maple from Japan, a cactus from Bermuda. The orchid house held many interesting specimens, rare in this country.

You could have seen peaches and nectarines in profusion in another hothouse; pineapples there were, too, and the fine banana plant in July, 1904, had six rows of bananas formed. In the vinery were plentiful bunches of ripening grapes.

In a special span-roofed greenhouse containing cactus curiosities an African plant suspended from the roof was famous because it required only air for its sustenance, bearing beautiful blue flowers in return. Elsewhere, a night-flowering cactus had borne as many as twenty-one blooms. In the delightful fernery trailing plants transformed the walls and roof into a delicate tracery of beauty, and the passion flower and climbing plants trained along the roof provided a " feast for the eye,"

A rose house produced an abundant variety for your delight, and a rich wealth of colour greeted you in the petunia and geranium greenhouse. Hydrangeas carrying magnificent heads of blue blooms, fuschias and lemon-centred verbenas shared a house with arum lilies and eucalyptus in good display.

Before you left the gardens you would be shown the tulip tree and the magnolia. And the most precious plant in the gardens you would certainly already have seen—the famous " filmy fern " from New Zealand, declared to be the only one in England when Mr. John Waterhouse introduced it here in 1860.

What happened to this fern, how it was offered to the King, its adventures in the transfer to Kew Gardens from Well Head, are worth recalling on another occasion. It is safe to say that when you finally left the gardens you would find it impossible to believe that what you had seen flourished so near the heart of industrial Halifax!

Fern that made history.

TWELVE thousand miles it had travelled to Mr. John Waterhouse's gardens at Well Head, Halifax, that " filmy " fern he had ordered in 1860 from its native New Zealand forest. And although the fern was said to be at least 150 years old when it undertook the journey it was by no means at the end of its adventures. When it arrived here it was already famous, for it was the first to be introduced into England, it was stated; but it was to become more renowned still.

The lacy, delicate, almost transparent fronds of this great fern— " Todea Superba," to do it the justice of giving it its proper name— were four or five feet in length. The plant required copious watering three times daily on the voyage, and this was continued in its new home here.

In New Zealand, the fern had been growing deep down in a gully where the sun never penetrated and where a splashing stream flung spray over it continuously. At Well Head a glass case about eight feet square was erected to conserve moisture. Accompanying it in its greenhouse were snow-white clematis and passion flowers that had grown in the forest above the same dark gully, and several other rare ferns had been brought over at the same time.

For fifty-six more years the plant was cared for and admired with all the other horticultural treasures at Well Head. Then, in 1916, came the sale of the greenhouses and their contents, after the death of Mrs. Doherty Waterhouse. But Todea Superba was not for sale : its rarity, its venerable age and its delicate beauty rendered it " fit only for a king," as one admirer recorded it—and to King George V. it was offered. Soon afterwards, the fern had embarked on another journey, to the Royal Botanical Gardens at Kew.

Elaborate were the precautions against damage in transit. The Well Head gardeners accompanied the plant, which by arrangement with the railway company travelled in a truck attached to a slow train to lessen the likelihood of jolting. On route it had its waterings and was watched over with the greatest care. Four gardeners from Kew were on the platform awaiting the fern's arrival in London, with a vehicle to carry it to the gardens, where a special " house " had been prepared to receive it.

To-day (nearly forty more years having elapsed) there is in the filmy fern house at Kew, " one large Todea Superba," and six rare ferns recorded as from the Waterhouse collection may also be seen there.

Buffalo Bill's Wild West Show.

OF all the outdoor shows that toured the world half a century ago, none was more famous or a greater attraction than Buffalo Bill's Wild West Show—and no other show that visited Halifax could have found the weather such an enemy and a handicap! "It could not have been worse," said the "Guardian," reporting the events on Skircoat Moor of October 8, 1903. Early in the morning, three special trains on the High Level Railway had brought to Pellon Station the unfamiliar cargo of people and horses making up the teams, and had disembarked them before most of the townsfolk were awake. To "the Moor" the cavalcade tramped and rode in the pouring rain, those American cow-boys, Mexican rough-riders, Cossacks, Arabs and Indians, with their spirited animals, and on the sodden Moor they raised their camp. So many were there that the feeding of the encamped performers under such dreadful conditions won the admiration of the spectators.

The "Congress of Rough Riders of the World," as the show was also styled, triumphed over the elements, however, and drew large crowds to two performances in spite of the chilly discomfort of the perpetual rain that turned the ground into a quagmire. Two powerful searchlights failed to brighten the scene owing to the heavy mist rising from the drenched ground, and the effect at the night performance was very weird, we are told, in the steely glitter of the electric lights. But the continual downpour did not rid the galloping steeds of their mettle nor the courageous riders of their pluck, and the full planned programme from the opening to the final review was carried through. As the rough-riders dashed about the enclosure they yelled their pulse-stirring cries and lightened the gloom with bright flashes of colour. The lassoing of the cowboys was "like a fine art." There were the emigrant trains crossing the plains, the attack on the settlers' camp, and the dramatic repulse of the attackers by a posse of soldiers. The military gave exciting exhibitions, too, and novel life-saving apparatus was brought into play. The bivouacs and the camp fires gave a fascinating realism to the events, and the war dance of the Indians was pronounced the most exciting in its novelty.

This Wild West Show of Buffalo Bill's, with its contingents from the East, brought the rough life of the plains and the steppes and the deserts to Halifax with a vengeance that day, and the pitiless rain could not damp the admiration of the thousands of soaked spectators.

Houdini at People's Palace.

HALIFAX people flocked to " The People's Palace " (one of many temporary titles enjoyed by the Odd Fellows' Hall) during a week in October, 1902, to see the " famous American gaolbreaker and hand-cuff king of the world," who headed the list of artistes.   For it was well known that Houdini had defied the efforts of all the chief detective forces, including Scotland Yard, to handcuff him in such a manner as to prevent him getting free.   It also became known that on the Monday morning Houdini had visited police headquarters, that he had been securely handcuffed by police officers there, and that he had extricated himself in a remarkable manner.

On the stage, various kinds of handcuffs and leg chains were assembled.   The military brought some from their collection at the Barracks and the police produced more for the occasion, but Houdini freed himself from all these obstacles with dramatic effect and without real difficulty.   Any contraption that the town or the audience could devise was welcome to Houdini.   He extricated himself from a strait-jacket; he was manacled, and was fastened in all kinds of ways, but it made little difference what iron or steel or wooden apparatus was introduced—he made short work of them all.

A member of the audience, proud of his skill in knotting ropes with patent knots that could not be undone without cutting, with great pains bound Houdini to a ladder—but his victim released himself in just half the time it had taken to fasten him up !   The following month, during a return week's appearance at the People's Palace, Houdini was engaged for a special Saturday display at the new Victoria Hall, supported by an augmented company of artistes.   The sensation he had created during his earlier visit brought the crowds again to see the man.

In addition to repeating other popular achievements, he was put in a locked packing case specially made by a local contractor.   This, it was reasonable to suppose, would have silenced him for ever—for a stipulation was that Houdini had to get himself out without injuring the case or the ropes that bound it.   Intense excitement held the audience as they waited, it was reported.   But Houdini, after twenty-two minutes, liberated himself, amid resounding cheers, and appeared to have enjoyed his temporary banishment.   As a variant to these exhausting feats, he entertained the audience by performing several clever illusions.

9

The tram mail wagon.

WHEN it emerged from the Halifax General Post Office on July 31, 1902, after experimental journeys, the new tramway mail wagon was announced to be unique as a vehicle. It had been designed and constructed in Halifax, was approved by the Postmaster General, the Board of Trade and the Town Council. Its purpose was to convey the mail between the Post Office and the station, and the truck was so designed that it left the Post Office loaded with its parcels and mailbags, and was trundled to the electric tram track in Commercial Street, where it was attached to a tramcar that would take it via Ward's End to the bottom of Horton Street.

Its useful journey did not end there, however, for the main advantage of this novel wagon was that it would deliver its load directly into the railway mail van from the Post Office without intermediate transhipment or handling of the mails. At the station approach the vehicle was detached from the tram, manhandled into the station and run straight into the luggage lift. Having descended to the platform it was wheeled to the side of the train mail van and its contents were unloaded, the reverse process operating for inward mails. The truck itself was just short of six feet in length, had strong wicker sides and base, its framework being painted a bright Post Office vermillion that gave it a very smart appearance, and it bore the Royal Cipher at each end. At this time the electric trams themselves were still only a four-year-old novelty and the mail wagon was an early enterprising development, in which the town took a justifiable pride. Changes during the past half-century have speeded up the transport to and from the station, but no system introduced has eliminated the manhandling of the mails there as did this tramways truck.

There were not many miles of track for the electric trams in 1902, but just at the time the mail wagon was introduced a curious—and nowadays incredible—"burden" on the Corporation was reported. Fares from the tramcars had imposed an unforseen penalty: a quarter of a million pennies and halfpennies were amassed at the Town Hall—coins which the local banks would not take. The Corporation had no choice but to announce its predicament in the " Courier " and to suggest that shopkeepers and other traders might be disposed to exchange this thousand pounds hoard for more negotiable currency!

The Salterhebble "lift".

TRAMS deriving current from overhead wires or from underground cables were "considered preferable to those with large unsightly steam engines or with the hard trot of horses on our stone paving. To have cars of a neat description like Mr. Smith's of Bradford, running almost noiselessly through the town to the suburbs would be a boon . . ." This problem of the form of electric tram Halifax should adopt occupied the council in 1892. The overhead wires won, and from 1898 the new tram routes steadily extended to the outskirts. Salterhebble Hill alone remained an obstacle.

In 1902, the necessity of serving the population of West Vale and beyond—and a proposal, approved, to extend the tramways from Stump Cross to Hipperholme—exercised a council meeting for several hours. A strong argument for both extensions was the large supply of rails and poles and other "unremunerative stock—£30,000 worth deteriorating for want of using." Salterhebble Hill could not be negotiated by trams, some councillors maintained, without risk of accidents and certain shattering of the strongest nerves. But an alternative was debated, and it had ardent supporters.

This was a "lift" or balanced tramway down the Dudwell cliff side. The tram-lines from Skircoat Green would be extended into Dudwell Lane and across the field near the school to the cliff edge. The foot of the lift would be within easy approach to the West Vale road, where journeys by tram would be resumed. Two engines, drivers and gatemen would be required. Four journeys an hour would effect a saving of 6d. a car, or £620 per annum, over the "long route by Salterhebble Hill," the engineer estimated. Cart traffic would be carried by the lift, much traffic from Sowerby Bridge via Wakefield Road being expected, to avoid the climb to King Cross. It would lift 120 loads a day at 4d. a load; whereas it cost waggoners 6d. to hire a chain horse to assist loads up Salterhebble Hill. But £4,000 had been expended on improving and widening the hill in readiness for the tramways. Many were the arguments for and against both schemes.

Finally, a London civil engineers was engaged to advise which scheme would be the better, safer and most economical. He was met at the station by the Corporation wagonette, driven to Salterhebble to inspect the hill and the selected lift-bottom position, whence he walked up the slope to the proposed starting point by Dudwell Gate, and he was in his train for London three hours after arrival . . . The lift was forgotten; and for 35 years trams ran up and down Salterhebble Hill, carrying millions of passengers without accident.

Command Performance.

WHEN a brass band strikes up a lively tune in the street at five in the morning you may be sure something is afoot. And when this happened in Queen's Road on August 10, 1902, it announced that the King Cross Band was marching to the Trafalgar Inn, where a reception and a large " Welcome " banner awaited it. For almost a week, crowned by its Command Performance at Buckingham Palace the day before the Coronation of King Edward VII. the band had kept up a triumphal progress of engagements in London—the " climax of their successes," the " Courier " reporter described the visit.

At performances in the Victoria Embankment Gardens and in St. James's and other parks during the week the band had audiences varying between ten thousand and thirty thousand people, it was reported. A speech was called for at one concert, and the band secretary, Mr. H. Bennett, responded. A special performance was given in the gardens for Pressmen, who gave the band highest praise.

On the Friday came the summons to the Palace. First the band played " inside the railings," while a large crowd assembled outside; then it was escorted to an inner quadrangle and there formed up for playing. The King appeared at a window, bowed to the bandsmen, and the conductor, Mr. W. Clegg, raised his baton for the selected renderings from Sullivan's operas, following with Gounod's " Faust " and the National Anthem.

After His Majesty's acknowledgment of enjoyment the bandsmen were conducted into the Palace to partake of hospitality and to inspect the Royal apartments. The next day they watched the Coronation procession leave the Palace, having splendid views of the pageantry. At night, they were entertained by the suppliers of their instruments before being driven to King's Cross for their night train.

On June 21, 1911, the band was again playing at Buckingham Palace by Royal command, for the Coronation of King George V and Queen Mary. Their smart appearance in their best uniforms and with their shining instruments, as they played during luncheon to fifty diplomatic representatives where the Guards' bands normally played, received great acclamation from the crowds deeply lining the railings.

An artistic decorated programme containing a photograph of the bandsmen and inscribed with their names was presented to Their Majesties. They received the congratulations of the King, who, in response to his inquiry about the bandsmen, was told by the Deputy Mayor, Mr. G. T. Ramsden, that they had been at their work the day before and had travelled overnight. Queen Mary also expressed her pleasure personally. The band was then entertained to lunch at the Palace. It travelled back to Halifax in the night, arriving in the early morning, but again played at King Cross before disbanding.

"The Southowram Light Railway"

THE railway that might have been—but for the obstacles which so often prevent the carrying-out of projects when plans have been made for their fulfilment. Half a century ago Southowram was in the peculiar position of being surrounded by a largely unexploited wealth of stone, fireclay and, it was believed, coal, yet suffering, owing to its lofty situation, from lack of communication with the valley railways, so near and yet so far, encircling Beacon Hill. Horse and wagon transport of the heavy production from the quarries to the stations at North Bridge, Elland and Brighouse was cumbersome and costly. The population was declining because of the little township's disadvantages.

Two schemes for connecting Southowram with the main lines were planned, and finally in 1901 they were submitted to the Light Railway Commissioners. One was to link the hilltop with Elland, and it encompassed the incredible drop in level of 500 feet in the space of a few miles. The other would connect with the new High Level Railway at Holmfield.

At a three-day inquiry in the Victoria Hall between the Earl of Jersey, with a representative of the Commissioners, and the legal advocates of the local promoters, the Elland line project (opposed by the Great Northern Railway) was rejected. But the plan for the line to Holmfield was considered flavourably, and when the details had been thrashed out was sanctioned provisionally. It was estimated that 200,000 tons of load would be carried annually, and the Lancashire and Yorkshire Railway also would benefit greatly. Amazing though it appears when viewing the contours inexpertly, the 4¾-mile line as planned from Southowram to Holmfield had few gradients of more than 1 in 50, and it was fairly direct. From Milking Hill, the proposed starting point, the route crossed Church Lane and followed the eastern flank of Beacon Hill, across Lister's Road, over Godley Cutting to Horley Green and Claremount, passing under Boothtown Road near the New Delight Inn and terminating near Churn Milk Lane at Holmfield. The Commissioners intimated after the inquiry that the application was granted, subject to confirmation by the Board of Trade and to the acceptance of terms by persons concerned in the line of route.

But there was to be no railway for Southowram, and Milking Hill and Churn Milk Lane remained as refreshingly pastoral as their singularly twin-like names. It was probably fortunate for the railway's prospects that the obstacles frustrated construction—for while they developed so was the infant (and unforseen) motor transport developing and coming to the rescue of Beacon Hill and its valuable industry.

A " World's Fair " at Thrum Hall.

DURING a whole month in 1900 crowds came from near and far to Thrum Hall, and there must have been few Halifax people who did not join these visitors to the great " World's Fair, Carnival and Universal Exhibition " there. On the first Saturday alone there were 20,000 visitors. This enterprise of the Halifax Cricket and Football Club to raise funds could hardly have been excelled, and two years' work had gone into the preparations. Seven thousand pounds were required, £2,000 being for the new covered stand to replace a wooden erection—which some supporters of the old club may still remember.

The ground was transformed. A lake stretched almost the entire length of the field, and between this and the boundary wall stood an ambitious representation of old Pompeii, for a nightly spectacle that was " a marvellous and majestic sight such as had never been attempted outside London." This was only one of many novel attractions to draw the crowds to the exhibition, which had a serious business side for the town. The cycle track round the cricket enclosure was occupied by local tradespeoples' stalls. In the centre of the main ground was a bandstand where military and local bands entertained the crowds. Two fountains played in the lake; a " cinematograph show "—this, of course, a complete novelty then—drew large crowds, who saw local views and people on the screen.

Educated bears, snake charmers, acrobats, a rifle range, and other sideshows gave the World's Fair lively support. A popular balloonist made ascents from time to time throughout the Exhibition. A 150-feet-long dance floor was laid down on the football field, and fireworks displays followed the nightly variety shows given in the specially built theatre. Tea-rooms and buffets were there to refresh the visitors, who could rest in rustic summer-houses. For a month a veritable Earls Court could be explored for a humble shilling, the announcements said. The club's blue and white colours adorned the ground, which (only two decades after the first electric bulb appeared in Halifax) was lighted in the evenings by electricity.

The grand finale each day was the destruction of Pompeii, when the town, revealed by the tableaux beyond the lake at the height of its " wickedness," was destroyed by the burning lava flowing from Mount Vesuvius in the background. A thrilling spectacle, this, in which 350 people took part on the 350-foot stage, and a choir of 200 local voices sang. Nightly the Pompeii revellers were saved for the next night's spectacular production—for the boats on the 300-feet-long sheet of water in front of the stage were in readiness to give them refuge.

The trestle bridge at Blake Dean

RECENT enough to be remembered by many, but unseen by anyone since 1912, was the remarkable structure that came into being with the construction of the three Walshaw Dean reservoirs. The unique wooden trestle bridge carried the light railway 700 feet across the Hardcastle Crags valley from the Blake Dean road, and from the opposite hillside the line climbed through the tortuous cutting and over the bracken-covered moorland to the reservoir sites. The bridge was 105 feet above the stream; it was in three tiers, its central section resting on massive stone foundations, the ends of the three spans anchored in the widening sides of the valley. With its locomotives and trains of trucks continually crossing during the seven years of reservoir construction, the scene was transformed into one of noisy activity. A works line of rails also ran for a short distance alongside the stream.

Over the bridge passed much of the material to feed the immense undertakings that were in progress out on the Walshaw watershed. At one period 600 men were employed there, and they mostly lived during this time in a temporary hut-village known locally as " Dawson City," near Heptonstall. Engines whistled and trains rattled over the bridge with wagons packed with workmen, many of them Irish, going to and from their labours, sitting in dangerous positions with their legs dangling over the truck sides or perched on the square wooden buffers. On the trucks sometimes were old horse-trams, still labelled with their former destinations, that were being taken up to the workings for cabins in the moorland wilderness. The track crossed gullies in places and negotiated hilly and swampy ground in turns. The cutting that carried the line from the bridge past Blake Dean, and some other sections of the route, may still be traced, and the stone supports still stand in the valley.

The bridge was dismantled in 1912, five years after the opening of the reservoirs, when it became insecure. Soon after demolition began an engine left the rails near Clough Hole, two and a half miles from " Dawson City," ploughed through the embankment and plunged over the edge of the steep Hardcastle slope, where it stuck against a tree. The driver was saved by wire netting protecting the line, and thirty men in a truck escaped injury as their vehicle kept the rails.

In the serenity and beauty of Blake Dean today, where the twin streams from Widdop and Walshaw meet, it seems impossible that all this was happening there less than half a century ago.

Pictures at Fair caused a sensation.

WHETHER there were " horror comics " circulating locally half a century ago or not, there were people in Halifax who took strong exception to certain pictures that were shown at the Fair in June, 1898. There was no British Board of Film Censors for the " biographs " of those days; but feeling ran high here on this occasion and produced declarations that some of the pictures and posters were " unfit for public exhibition." One objector gave publicity to his opinions anonymously in the local paper. This promoted a violent reaction—and threats against the accuser, to be carried out if only his name and address could be discovered.

So incensed were the showmen that they staged a Sunday meeting in protest against the allegations. A reverend gentleman was present whom the showmen claimed was their chaplain, and he publicly denied that anything objectionable was ever shown. He declared he would have resigned office had it been otherwise.

A great surprise was in store for the " excited crowd of four hundred mostly showmen." For in their midst was a journalist, who jumped to his feet unexpectedly and announced that he was the writer of the anonymous protest. Despite the shaking fists, we are told, he delivered a scathing denunciation; and he also drew from the " chaplain " an admission that he had not seen the film pictures which had led to the controversy. The outcome of this meeting, at which the journalist scored heavily, was that the town authorities took up the matter.

The Chief Constable was notified, and two detectives were sent to visit the Fair to see if there was ground for the allegations. These officers, we learn from the report, while amused by some of them, did not find either the films or the other pictures complained of objectionable. To verify the opinions of the police officers, a councillor and the Markets Inspector visited the show. They, too, appreciated the amusement value, but some of the pictures might be open to objection, they decided. At their request, certain of them were withdrawn from the exhibition.

But the showmen refused to remove poster pictures from outside the cinematograph show that were pronounced " suggestive." The inspector and his colleague agreed that " whether they were immoral depended on the eye of the beholder." The council had no power to enforce their withdrawal : the same posters had been exhibited all over the country and Halifax was the first place to complain, said the showmen. They consented, however, to give certain of these posters less prominence. In the end a Morals Sub-Committee was appointed which had the duty of seeing all pictures and films before exhibition at future Fairs.

Sudden shock sensations.

THERE was just as good a chance in the more leisurely days of the last century of meeting with sudden calamity, shock, or unexpected sensation while pursuing one's daily round as there is today. On June 4, 1897, for instance, a hairdresser was walking with his wife along Commercial Street, Halifax, at 11-30 p.m., towards their home in Crown Street. As they passed the Lancashire and Yorkshire Bank building, a thirty-pound stone ball fell from its roof pinnacle, catching our unfortunate twonsman a glancing blow. Both he and his wife narrowly escaped severe injury.

No cause for the stone's fall was discovered; there was no wind, and the building was comparatively new. What happened to the victim makes strange reading today. Without waiting for the ambulance that had been sent for passers-by improvised a stretcher with their walking-sticks, the patient's home being so near, and his wife not wanting him to be taken to the Infirmary!

A shock of a different kind assailed people who chanced to be in Silver Street on March 15, 1888, shortly after an outbreak of fire at an ironmonger's premises. Several pounds of gunpowder stored in the building suddenly exploded with a terrific report that seemed to shake the district. Large stones were hurled across into the open space at Cow Green, and windows at the Lord Nelson and King's Head Inns and at still more distant places were broken. Damage was extensive and the explosion was heard over a wide area.

Digging in a field adjoining his home at Illingworth, in September, 1832, the toiler had no reason to suppose his innocent task would produce a major sensation. Coming into contact with some bones, he sought his son's assistance, and together they unearthed a human skeleton. Excitement locally was intense, and the news spread. Multitudes visited the scene; the skeleton's teeth, which were in an excellent state of preservation, were " taken away by a curious person," the " Halifax Express " reported. " Curious " seems to be the right word ! The rest of the skeleton was interred in Illingworth Church graveyard.

What mystery there was about this unexpected discovery was explained, it seems, to everybody's satisfaction. About fifty years earlier a Scots pedlar had disappeared suddenly from the neighbourhood, and it was supposed had been murdered. It was, therefore, surmised that this skeleton of the " young man of large and muscular frame " was his. An interesting theory in the report that corroborated this idea was that the skull was of " that peculiar form usually assigned to the native of North Britain."

Calamity in Church Street.

SEEN from the Halifax Station approach in 1861 the great new building at Horton Street and Church Street corner must have appeared very striking. India House it was named by its inspirer, an export merchant trading with the East. It still bears its stone " world " over the corner entrance.

But only thirty-four years after its erection a catastrophe occurred at India House. Let us recall those few incredible minutes as they affected Mr. Bottomley, a cigar manufacturer, whose factory occupied part of the building.

At 6 p.m., after a business journey, Mr. Bottomley drove down Horton Street in his brougham intending to pick up his son at his office and to take him home. His workpeople had left, as had those of other tenant firms. His coachman stopped at the office door in Church Street and Mr. Bottomley entered his premises. He found that his son had gone, and he was about to return to the brougham when he went back into the office for a newspaper from his desk.

During those few seconds as he turned back he heard a heavy rumbling high above him, followed immediately by a tremendous crash in the street. He rushed to the entrance and was almost stunned by the sight that met him. Church Street was strewn with huge stones for the whole length of the building, the sight being so indescribable that it was some moments before Mr. Bottomley, as he said afterwards, " came to his senses." He realised then that the coachman and his horse and brougham, outside the door a minute before, were nowhere to be seen. They had been completely buried by the heavy stones. The entire length of overhanging coping stonework and cornices on the Church Street frontage had crashed to the ground without warning.

He remembered calling out : " Where is my poor coachman?" but he could only concern himself, like other people who were assembling, with the possibility of more deaths under the tons of stones. The noise, heard in the station, had been alarming, and the stationmaster at once sent his staff to help in searching the debris. It was not known how many pedestrians had been caught. Stones weighing five or six hundred-weights had to be shifted before the bodies of the coachman and the horse were discovered. The carriage had been crushed to matchwood.

There were no other fatalities, an amazing piece of good fortune considering the time at which the calamity had occurred. Mr. Bottomley owed his life to the impulse to slip back for his newspaper.

A picture of the building after the fall reveals what a weight of masonry was torn from it. Thus, today, India House shows a very different " sky-line " to anyone who looks upwards when passing in Church Street, from that which graced it just before 6 p.m. on October 16, 1895.

The Borough Markets.

THE central section of Halifax was completely transformed towards the end of last century by the erection of the Borough Market. The undertaking was a big one, entailing the clearing of the extensive and largely built-on area between Market Street and Southgate, widening the latter roadway, and demolishing many buildings, including the smaller market erected in 1810. With the cost of the land and the properties to be bought the scheme cost £105,000—a great sum in 1892. At a special ceremony on October 6 in that year the memorial stone of Aberdeen grey granite, bearing a tablet which records the names of Town Council members identified with the scheme, was placed inside the central Southgate entrance. For the occasion a mallet made of wood from a 200-year-old house demolished in the process of the site development was used.

Early in the century, the local marketing and open-stall trading arrangements were very crude and unhygienic compared with the new amenities. Sheep were slaughtered in some cases in front of the butchers shops. Water was not "on tap" for swilling, although the town was plentifully supplied with wells. Swine Market, Cow Green, Bull Green and Corn Market, were all marketing centres where buying and selling were allowed for six hours one day a week, on market day. Then came the early market building, improved facilities, piped water, sanitation and separate places for slaughter; and the Lower Market provided many stalls and stands in an enclosed and spacious covered building. With the erection of the handsome Borough Market building, with its arcade and eight entrance gateways, the last word in covered markets had arrived.

On July 25, 1896, the Duke and Duchess of York came to Halifax on a State visit to declare open the market and the new Halifax Infirmary. The town gave itself up to high festivity and to acclaiming the future King George V. and Queen Mary. After a reception at the Town Hall and a luncheon with 240 guests at Belle Vue, the Duke and Duchess formally opened the infirmary, using an 18-carat gold key ornamented with the Halifax coat-of-arms, which was presented to the Duke. Afterwards, the Royal party went to the new market, where a great crowd had assembled, entertained by the Lee Mount Band playing in one of the balconies. The formal opening ceremony then took place. Their Royal Highnesses later passed under a triumphal arch erected across Horton Street on their way to rejoin the then famous Great Northern Royal saloon coach at the station.

Night Drama at Blackstone Edge

A MAN entered the deserted bar of the Waggon and Horses Inn (now the White House Inn) at Blackstone Edge on the evening of December 6, 1894, and asked for threepennyworth of whisky. His questioning of the girl who served him led her to fetch Mrs. McIntyre, the landlord's wife. She, too, became suspicious of his appearance and of his questions, and called her husband. During conversation McIntyre passed through the bar towards the kitchen, and found the customer following with a revolver pointed at him. As he turned the man fired, and the bullet penetrated his shoulder. His wife rushed from the kitchen to the assailant, who immediately fired at her. The steel of her corset deflected the shot and saved her from injury. She staggered with her injured husband into the kitchen and they blocked the door against the would-be murderer, who shouted and threatened.

McIntyre's wound was bleeding profusely, and he was in great pain, but with his wife and the servant he climbed through a window and escaped on to the moor. There they lay concealed, watching. The nearest habitation was a mile away, and the moorland was deserted on this mid-winter night. The girl became frightened, refused to stay, and ran towards the road. But the man had emerged from the inn, and he saw her. He caught her, and threatened to kill her unless she told him where the inn money was kept. Mr. and Mrs. McIntyre saw him return to the house, and the girl run down the hill.

Shortly afterwards, a trap in which were two men who had been out shooting drew up the road. Mrs. McIntyre stopped it, told her story to the occupants, who took her to the mile-distant farm—her father's, where they found the girl—and then went to Littleborough with the news. They returned with medical help for the landlord, still lying injured on the moor, and police arrived from Littleborough in a hansom. They found the inn rooms ransacked, but some items of value, including £50 and a gold watch, had been overlooked. The man had vanished.

The police acted promptly. Warnings were sent to Halifax, Todmorden and Huddersfield, and all roads from the moors were watched. The next morning, police surprised the fugitive near the Derby Bar, above Rishworth. His five-chambered revolver was in his pocket, fully loaded. He was taken to Rochdale, charged the following day with attempted murder, and removed to Strangeways Gaol to await trial. The landlord's wound was serious, his arm bone had been splintered; but the bullet was extracted, and he recovered. The girl refused to return to the Inn.

When the lion got out at Halifax Fair.

THE liveliness and gaiety of the Fair in Halifax on that Thursday evening in June of 1893, was suddenly changed to excitement and panic.

The escape of a full-grown lion from the menagerie at the Victoria Fairground created pandemonium. Orenzo, a black lion-tamer, entered " Nero's " cage as usual at 8-15 p.m. " Nero " crouched and instantly sprang at him, taking him off his guard while the cage gate was still open. While Orenzo was on the ground, " Nero " escaped and bounded at large among the fairground shows.

There were injuries to people scrambling for safety : hats and bonnets were lost or crushed. A man at whom the lion sprang had his face clawed and his clothes torn. As he ran away in his fright, " Nero " followed and attacked him again, wounding him in the right leg, before bounding off. Another man was forced against a swinging "boat," suffering a fractured skull and a dislocated jaw.

Meanwhile, " Nero," wild with fright himself, ran underneath a platform of one of the shows. Kept imprisoned there by boards held round it, he was driven gradually under the steps leading to the platform. Onlookers were invited to stand on the steps to keep them weighted down. Various attempts at capture, including efforts with a carrying cage, were fruitless.

Orenzo was about again, and he had to show " Nero " who was master. After several vain attempts he managed, through a space between the steps, to slip a looped rope over the lion's head, and at the right moment pulled the rope tight. The slip-knot loop held " Nero " firm. There was loud praise and applause from the crowd.

The lion appeared to be exhausted; the rope was so tight he could scarcely breathe. But when the trainer tried to ease the rope, " Nero " clawed him and tried to bite his leg. Lifting the presently almost inanimate body of the lion on to a stout board, with ropes, was safely accomplished, and on this he was carried to his cage. " Nero " lay there as if dead. Buckets of water and loosening of the rope when he was secured revived him, however. And he performed again the following day.

At the inquiry, Orenzo told of a previous escape of " Nero " into the streets of Birmingham, when with Wombwell's menagerie. There he had chased the lion with a boar-hound—and had captured him in a sewer. Orenzo took him back to his cage in a " trap," and received £200 as a reward from Wombwell's. A medal was also struck for him by a grateful Birmingham.

"The Twelve Apostles"

FEW greater transformations can have been effected anywhere by the construction of a new roadway than that created little more than half a century ago by the new Skircoat Road. Previously, the town's southern outlets had been Shaw Hill and the pretty lane leading through the fields in the valley towards Free School Lane, known as Caygill's Walk.

The depression in the ground beginning about Bell Hall, skirting Rothwell Road, then sloping down through Well Head fields and deepening all the way down to Shaw Hill and as far as the Hebble, was crossed about midway by this new direct roadway from the centre of the town. Begun in 1890, the work was a major operation in construction, involving building the long embankment across the valley, forty feet high in places; the thousands of tons of material had all to be brought from a distance to its position. The levelling of what is now the Shay football ground below also produced problems and much Council disputation about letting the space to contractors for tipping—as did the built-up ground soon to be used for the new tram depot.

One branch of the new highway met the road to Huddersfield at the top of Shaw Hill, the other curving up to Free School Lane. These new sections enclosed a triangular plot of land on which stood the old Heath Hall.

This is where we meet the " Twelve Apostles "—a dozen large trees that spread their leafy branches over the lane leading from Free School Lane to Caygill's Walk as it left the valley. The Heath Road fork and the development of the enclosed Heath Hall estate by builders sealed the doom of the " Apostles." One by one they disappeared.

Ten years after the Skircoat Road was begun there were still two of these trees standing, but their time soon came. Local attachment for these fine old trees prompted an attempt to save the last one. It was transplanted in the laid-out corner ground enclosed by the road fork, which shortly after became known as Albert Park when the statue of the Prince Consort on his horse was transferred here from Horton Street in 1902. But the tree did not survive, and all trace of the old " Twelve Apostles " vanished.

When the road-making project was in its early stages it was proposed that a 44-foot cross road midway between the fork and Free School Lane should divide the plot, connecting Skircoat Road and Heath Road, and should be named Godfrey Road. This plan did not mature, and Godfrey Road appeared later at Skircoat Green.

"Heir to four million pound estate!"

A STORY of fact more fantastic than the most romantic fiction is recorded in connection with Ovenden Hall. It developed in the fertile mind of a young man who, in the last century, leaving work in Halifax for employment elsewhere, lodged in a house where he formed an attachment for his landlord's young daughter. His romance soon became complicated, for, being out of funds, he induced the young lady to lend him money—money that had been entrusted to her by her father. One inducement was his assurance that, being the heir to Ovenden Hall in Halifax, he would inherit a large fortune very shortly—on his twenty-first birthday.

The young man was generous in the extreme in return for the total of £17 he acquired from this source. He gave the girl a sealed envelope, which, he told her, contained his will; this, he said, made over to her the entire Ovenden Hall estate and the fortune attached to it. He produced for the enlightenment of his fortunate young friend—and of her father, who had become interested in his unusual lodger—photographs of the Hall, showing a long carriage drive, gardens with impressive statuary, a fish pond and other attractive features.

It appeared from the girl's evidence in court when eventually the romancer found himself under trial for procuring money by false pretences, that he had told her the estate was worth four million pounds. It also appeared from the case report that loud laughter in court was difficult to silence as her story unfolded. For one thing, the sealed envelope had contained only a blank sheet of paper, she had found. And for another, when the accused had taken her to call upon his lawyer to show how genuine was his claim to the estate, that gentleman was found to be away: he had gone over to Ovenden Hall, explained her escort on emerging from the office, to visit other solicitors from London in connection with his coming-of-age title to the estate. He thereupon offered to marry her three days after his twenty-first birthday to put everything in order.

The court heard the agent for the owner of Ovenden Hall declare that the photographs showed a mansion in no aspect recognisable as the Hall—which had no long carriage drive, no fish pond he had yet discovered, and as for the statuary . . . .

The accused admitted the stories he had told were wholly false. The chairman said to him: "You are one of those foolish youths whose head is filled with nonsense through reading 'penny dreadfuls'." Hard work was what *he* needed; and the sentence was four months hard labour.

The High Level Railway.

THE brand-new stations at St. Paul's and Pellon on the High Level Railway in Halifax were scenes of rejoicing on September 4, 1890. The procession of the Mayoral party, directors of the High Level, Great Northern and Lancashire and Yorkshire Railways, the military, the police and representatives of trade and other organisations, arrived at St. Paul's at 2 p.m., headed by the fife and drum band of the Duke of Wellington's W.R. Volunteer Battalion. Guests and public on the platforms were awaiting the inaugural ceremony and the departure of the two trains standing in the station.

This was the culmination of an enterprise which had encountered opposition for seven years, yet was widely acclaimed when completed. It had been claimed that the saving in cartage alone would be £10,000 a year, heavy traffic for a growing manufacturing district having to be dragged 1½ miles up a 500-foot rise. Six hundred men had been engaged on the construction.

It was a costly stretch of railway, with cuttings, tunnel and viaduct on most of its three-mile route. The first sod had been cut by the Mayor, Alderman James Booth, nearly three years earlier, near Greystones, Wheatley, where was to be the mouth of the 800-yard tunnel dividing Wheatley and Ovenden. From St. Paul's the line was carried through a cutting almost parallel with Queen's Road to Pellon station, thence skirting the hillside and crossing the valley by a ten-arch viaduct, the central arch being 100 feet high. From the tunnel the line emerged below the Illingworth Road and continued to Holmfield, there linking up with the G.N. line to Bradford and Keighley. In his speech at the opening Dr. Bowman, vice-chairman of the new railway, reminded the spectators that one prominent Halifax citizen had so doubted the practicability of the enterprise that he would be prepared " to eat the first locomotive that entered the station up there." A fine one was ready here for him, he declared; if the gentleman began at the funnel end he might find it tough, but he would find the end tender !

With the Duke's band playing lively airs, the entraining proceeded, and as the decorated engine drew out the military guard presented arms. The tunnel entrance was barred, and a gold and silver key was presented to the Mayoress for a brief opening ceremony there, Lord de Ramsey, a Great Northern Railway director, leading her to the barricade. Then the train proceeded to Holmfield and returned, the second train meanwhile having set out. Pellon station was a nursery-garden station on that day. St. Paul's was the site of the Free Wanderers football ground.

When the women cricketers entertained.

THE twenty-two women drew large attendances at the Halifax Cricket and Football ground on August 20 and 21, 1890. They had been announced as "introducing the latest novelty in outdoor games" to Halifax. Their visit for a two-day cricket match was a fixture in their tour of the country lasting from April to October. Feminine spectators were greatly interested and amused, the "Halifax Guardian" reported. The players were wearing uniforms consisting of "a loose sailor-like bodice and a full skirt," and as the teams were named "Reds" and "Blues" respectively, the women wore caps of their team's colour.

They were no mean adepts at the game, we are told; their clever fielding put in the shade many cricketing teams which had appeared on the Halifax ground. They had had careful and thorough training by leading cricketers of the day. Their throwing-in was especially good, "there being no hesitating or doubts as to which wicket the ball ought to be thrown to," and the wicketkeepers received the balls thrown in in a manner which called forth loud applause.

One young lady caused great astonishment at the ease with which she stopped with her left hand possible boundaries, and several difficult catches were achieved by other fielders. The batting of the captain of the "Reds" was of quite a dashing nature, the reporter said; she had herself made 1,000 runs since the beginning of the tour, an average of fifty an innings, and both elevens had run up scores of two hundred at several matches. Here, "recent heavy rain" prevented a big score being made.

There was a very commendable difference between those cricketers and modern touring team players, apart from their sex. When "rain stopped play" it may have stopped their cricket, but it did not necessarily stop their entertaining. For they were most versatile visitors. On their second evening here they filled the Mechanics' Hall with an enthusiastic crowd, whom they delighted by a varied and attractive programme. There was a fencing encounter between two of the young ladies. A display of roller-skating followed, and so did vaulting and gymnastics, and vocal, concertina and other instrumental music—almost anything that could contribute to an enjoyable evening the "Blues" and "Reds" could provide. Of the group-singing it must be said in fairness to the loyal reporter that "it could be better done by the Halifax School Board children."

A surgery in a wagonette.

THE unbelieving called him a "quack doctor." But people went in thousands to see him working on patients in the Old Cattle Market in Gibbet Street for two weeks, in June, 1889. He was an American, known as "Sequah, the Rheumatic Doctor," and his visit was announced by a full page in the "Halifax Courier," strikingly set up and giving scores of testimonials from towns previously visited. "Sequah" moved about the town in style, driving in a well-appointed trap that was preceded by his small brass band riding in a wagonette. He began his sessions by addressing the gathering crowds from the wagonette. While his "cure" for sufferers from rheumatic complaints comprised medicine and liniment —a bottle of each for four shillings—"Sequah" had an entertaining routine that had to be gone through as a preliminary : he could sell his physic fast enough when the time arrived. First, his skill had to be demonstrated.

So up in the wagonette he extracted decayed teeth, a practice in which he was expert—and as he did this for nothing he did not lack customers. He would remove for anybody up to five or six teeth "painlessly" in half a minute. These operations were conducted in full view of the crowds who watched the novel entertainment. And the victims said the local reporter with grim humour, "walked off with their decayed grinders in their hats or bonnets, or down their backs "—for "Sequah" apparently had a playful way of keeping the performance amusing to the audience, on whom he counted for his sales. His band during these dental preliminaries "beguiled the time with sweet music."

Then came the turn of the rheumatic sufferers who had come to buy the curative physic. From them "Sequah" selected a bad case, who had to be lifted on to the wagonette to be treated. A rug was held discreetly round the old man whose ordeal is described, while he undressed. He was awarded a dose of the medicine, and then an Indian on "Sequah's" staff rubbed him with the liniment for half an hour. At the end of it, "Sequah" broke the old man's sticks, and his patient, "though stiff and sore, could walk freely, and gave a sort of shuffle meant for dancing," went off a happier man—who returned the next day with others to give testimony. Speculation as to whether the "cures" were permanent was plentiful; but hope of only temporary relief was enough to provide enormous custom for the bottles—and "Sequah" sold them as fast as they could be served out and for as long as he could receive the cash !

The Grand Theatre Opening.

ON the North Bridge site formerly occupied by the old Gaiety Music Hall the memorial stone-laying ceremony at the new Grand Theatre and Opera House provided Halifax with a much-heralded event on November 27th, 1888. The old Theatre Royal, it was said, would not accommodate sufficient people to enable the management to engage the best theatrical productions, and a town the size of Halifax could not, in any case, be satisfied by one theatre! So the Grand was designed by an architect of several London theatres at a cost of £16,000 to entertain 2,000 people (including 300 standing).

To perform the ceremony the eminent actor, Wilson Barrett, who had made his debut many years before in Halifax, came from Manchester, where he was fulfilling an engagement. He was met at the station by the Mayoral carriage and was entertained to luncheon at the Town Hall. There he was presented by the architect with a silver trowel which had his initials worked into its ivory handle, and by the local contractor with an ebony mallet similarly inscribed. The ceremony excited great interest. Wilson Barrett was popular here because of his fondness for and frequent association with the town, besides being nationally famous. Construction of the theatre was well advanced, and the memorial stone was lowered into a position where it could be read by many of the theatre's patrons. It bore the actor's name and those of the directors of the owning company. Barrett's final words after wishing prosperity to Halifax may fittingly be recalled, with the theatre's later difficulties in mind : " Long may this new theatre flourish and prosper. May it be so managed that it will prove a place where old and young, rich and poor may find forgetfulness of cares, help in their sorrows, instruction, relaxation, innocent recreation and amusement."

On August 5 the following year the Grand Theatre and Opera House was launched on its career by a three-play week. " Claudian," " Ben-my-Chree " and " Hamlet " were performed, Wilson Barrett playing the principal parts, with Miss Eastlake and George Barrett, both of the Princess Theatre (London) Company and others supporting. The opening was pronounced a " gigantic success." Thousands of delighted patrons that week exclaimed : " Oh ! What a lovely theatre !" we are told—a description publicly endorsed by Barrett himself on appearing before the curtain after the first performance of " Claudian," when he thanked the management and the people of Halifax for giving him the opportunity of opening their new theatre. Crowded houses were the rule for a long period, and this did not affect the audiences at the Theatre Royal in those early years. Many famous actors were seen at the Grand, including E. R. Benson in 1902 and Sir Henry Irving in 1903.

Eccentric Journeys.

WHETHER to win a bride, a wager, notoriety, even, or just for private satisfaction, local people in the past lacked nothing in eccentric ways of livening up life's routine. The two winsome women who were loved by one swain can be forgiven for their determination not to relinquish the loved one in favour of the rival; but it is startling to find that it was not the superior charms of one that won in the end, but prowess in running from the Horse and Jockey Inn, Elland, to the top of the Ainleys and back. This was why on September 10, 1881, the small one raced like a fury, outpaced her taller rival and qualified for matrimony with the heartless promoter of the contest!

When railway travel was more of a novelty, a local accountant set out to prove he could travel 1,000 miles by train in England in a day. Halifax-Leeds-King's Cross-St. Pancras-Carlisle-St. Pancras-King's Cross-Leeds-Halifax-the trains and timetables made it possible, the termini staffs certified his arrivals, and our railway enthusiast demonstrated his theory, reaching Halifax well within the twenty-four hours.

While we have the station in mind we might recall some minor excitement there on September 12, 1889. At 1 p.m. two expresses had left Bristol by different routes for Halifax and Bradford, the Midland train having two extra stops. At 5-57 p.m. the L. & N.W.R. train drew into Halifax, and the Midland train arrived three minutes later, promptly to time. A race of such a novel nature could be counted on to arouse excitement and cheers at the station even in the days of fast railway journeys.

As a change from running and railway travel there is the incredible walking achievement of the famous pedestrian, E. P. Weston, in 1879. When he strode into Halifax on St. Valentine's Day he had covered 1,441 miles since leaving the Royal Exchange, London, on January 18. His undertaking was to walk 2,000 miles and to deliver 50 lectures in as many different towns in 1,000 hours. His tour took him into thirty-one counties and 119 different towns. Three judges accompanied him —but their horses did the walking.

A very short journey provided sensation enough in a local hostelry, where a reckless customer wagered he could ascend to the roof via the fireplace and the flue. The landlord took charge of the stake money, and the climber disappeared up the chimney. There, out of sight, he stuck, and in his struggle he dislodge stones and loosened material. He reached the ground bruised and black with soot. The landlord claimed the money to pay for the repairs.

Early "Broadcasts" from Halifax

"THE system of speaking communication, by means of Crossley's Patent Transmitter, is now being established in Leeds, Bradford, Halifax and Huddersfield. The West Riding Telephone Company is now prepared to receive names of subscribers and to erect the necessary wires and instruments." So read an advertisement in a Yorkshire paper in August, 1879. The first public telephone service had just opened in London, Professor Graham Bell having startled the world by his invention of the telephone three years previously.

One of the new telephones had been installed in Dean Clough Mills, Halifax, in place of the private internal system that had been in use, this latter being largely the invention of Mr. Louis J. Crossley, of Moorside, formerly of Manor Heath. But the reception on the new Bell installation did not satisfy Mr. Crossley. He set himself to improve upon it, and the patent transmitter advertised was the result.

Within 12 months the telephone system which was put into operation in Halifax made use of this invention. For commercial usage the system was quickly recognised as being reliable and efficient: the "Crossley Transmitter" carried the message "more audibly to its destination." It was taken up on a wide scale. Mr. Crossley received for his patent £20,000 from the United Telephone Company, Ltd., who held the Bell the Edison and other patents, and he was recognised as being in the forefront of telephone development, achieving much deserved publicity in technical papers of the day.

Forty years in advance of radio broadcasting, Mr. Crossley installed a transmitter in Square Chapel to enable a service conducted by its re-nowned preacher, Dr. Mellor, to be received by means of his telephone system at the Congregational Chapel at Saltaire, and reporters stated that the sermon and the singing in Halifax could be heard "with great distinctness."

A further "broadcast" took place on February 1, 1881, when for demonstration to his audience at the Mechanics' Institute in Bradford, Mr. Walter Emmott, lecturing on "The Electrical Age," introduced by means of wires laid from Halifax a cornet solo, and singing and conversation, which were very clearly received. The striking of the Halifax Town Hall clock was also heard by this audience in Bradford 74 years ago.

While referring to Dr. Mellor, it is interesting to recall that in the grounds of his manse was a small platform, from which the preacher would board the trains which stopped to pick him up when he was making journeys westward along the line of the Lancashire and York-shire Railway, which ran at the foot of his garden.

Opposition to Halifax race meeting.

WHEN the Halifax Racing Company announced and advertised widely that the races would be held on July 14 and 15, 1879, the Mayor called a public meeting to consider their "effects and tendencies on the town." Opposition to the races was very strong on this occasion, for at the spring races dice gamblers and card sharpers had been active on the course. Protest notices were displayed; and a petition requiring the Mayor to call the meeting was alleged to have been signed by 723 burgesses. On the Sunday before the races the announcement of the special meeting had been conveyed to ministers with the request: "Please announce from the pulpit, morning and evening." But while some preached sermons against the racing, several ignored the request. The opponents proved to be a minority, and the case of the racing advocates was strengthened by the evidence they produced at the meeting that a big proportion of the signatories to the requisition were neither burgesses nor ratepayers.

So the races were held, and 81 horses ran on the racecourse at Highroad Well during those two days, a record for the course. They competed for more than £1,700 in prize-money—in the Prince of Wales's Stakes, the Calder Vale Handicap, a Tradesmen's Handicap, the Savile Park Plate, and several other races. Distinguished patrons with their ladies occupied the Steward's Box. And there was ample proof of the popularity of the races, for 20,000 people attended, in ideal weather.

As always in those days, when any special event called for it, the Lancashire and Yorkshire Railway rose to the occasion, and brought the crowds in their thousands in excursion trains from Manchester and many Lancashire towns, and from all over the West Riding. The Manchester, Sheffield and Lincolnshire Railway brought 300 from Sheffield. The excursion from Nottingham that brought 700 people must be recalled, for it was reported that "no more orderly or respectable excursion had been provided in connection with Halifax before." Some of the horses came from Newcastle and the Midland Counties.

This was the fourth meeting to be held on the racecourse. Altogether 254 horses had run to date, the value of the 46 prizes being £5,514. But patronage dropped off during the next five years, chiefly owing to the course being so far out of town and there being then no trams.

The last fixtures were in July, 1884. Thirty years later the grandstand was demolished and the stone used in the erection of the West End Golf clubhouse.

Floodlight football in 1878.

NOT to be outdone by other towns, Halifax was early in the field in in staging a novel football match when electric lighting was itself a novelty.

On November 2, 1878, the Halifax Cricket and Football Club, encouraged by the success and attraction of football matches by electric light at Bradford, Sheffield and Birmingham, arranged an evening match here with a team from Manchester, famous opponents on more normal occasions, known as " Birch." The home ground was in Hanson Lane.

Production of light was in the hands of Blakey Brothers and Emmott, electricians in the Square; and an illuminating angle on the event may be glimpsed by the report in the " Guardian " that " the inhabitants of the town were treated to a view of the light that is to work such a large revolution in the manufacture and sale of gas " !

At the kick-off at seven o'clock there was a large attendance, which increased as the lights attracted crowds of non-supporters to the match. Lights were placed behind the goalposts, worked by steam engines supplied by Messrs. Greenwood of Highroad Well; a third light at one side of the field, run by a battery, was intended to follow the movements of the players. Presumably it had its uses in enabling the players to see each other, and the ball, as well as to assist the twenty thousand people who had assembled by 7-40 p.m., when the lights were " turned on at full."

Keeping the ground clear seems to have been a major operation : when the length of the field was right the breadth of cleared space narrowed—or, as the reporter carefully stated, " was not according to rule."

The excitement of the crowd presently drove surging masses of people over the ground, scrummages among the spectators outshining anything the players could attempt, and finally obliterating their efforts completely. Strenuous attempts were made to clear the ground; but the crowd, we learn, was " stubborn," and both captains called their teams off the field.

Birch had come in their saloon carriage from Manchester, and had been rousingly cheered on arrival. They must have retreated thankfully to this carriage.

The " gate " receipts benefited the club's coffers by upwards of £250, but apparently the lights did not illuminate the gate pay boxes, for several thousand spectators succeeded in gaining admission without payment.

Northgate Surface Controversy.

NORTHGATE must hold prime place among Halifax Streets for problems it produces. At whatever period in its history it is observed, this most useful town artery has had its troubles. It has problems enough to-day connected with lights, traffic congestion, widening and property demolition; but one wonders what would be the reaction in the town now if shop-keepers in that contentious thoroughfare followed the example of their predecessors of the eighteen-seventies.

The street had been surfaced with granite setts in 1872. By 1877 the exasperation of the tradespeople in their dislike of this new surfacing method had reached explosion point. Every shopkeeper in Northgate signed a memorial complaining about the "noisy material" with which the street was paved and urging the Council to remove it and to repair the street with a less noisy surface. Five years was as long as they could put up with it.

So determined were they to be rid of the granite that they offered to enter into an agreement to pay part of the cost if the street could be re-paved with local stone. A deputation to the Board of Works suggested that the section from Woolshops to Crossley Street be relaid with stone setts as an experiment. Stone setts!

The Town Council held lengthy discussions on the matter. The Engineer estimated that a new stone surface on that section alone would cost £300, would last only five years, and that it would require £60 expending on it in repairs during the last two years of this period. The iron-shod wheels of the day would account for the rapid wear of the stone, as well as for the noise on the existing granite setts that the townspeople could bear no longer.

Loss of trade due to shoppers avoiding Northgate because of its dangerous surface; legs broken; injuries to health; jolts to the nervous system; horses thrown down; many were the arguments produced in the Council against the granite.

"Gentlemen would drive by a circuitous route rather than suffer the granite of Northgate," said the Councillor Longbottom of the day, who was wholeheartedly with the complainants. "Not until a gentleman of the Council happened an accident, got a leg broken, or was killed, or . . . until a bishop should stumble and fall, would the state of affairs be remedied," he added, drawing laughter by his fatalistic comment.

Northgate *was* re-paved, in due course, and this in spite of the absence of reported accidents to Councillors or to a bishop. But many further discussions and protests about the road surface intervened in more urgent matters before the local stone setts replaced the offending granite.

The opening of Ripponden Railway.

THIRTY years was a long time to wait for the branch railway to Ripponden from Sowerby Bridge. But reasons for its long-postponed construction by the Lancashire and Yorkshire Railway became clear to the Ryburn Valley population when the work was at last undertaken. It proved a dangerous and expensive enterprise. The railway's course of under four miles took five years to complete; and when it was opened, on August 5, 1878, 18 years had elapsed since the Act of Parliament authorising it. The line was intended to be continued beyond Ripponden, reports said, and was eventually to pass under Blackstone Edge into Lancashire; but extension was abandoned when this first section, now itself silent and deserted, was completed.

The danger was due to repeated landslides, some on a tremendous scale, which occasioned great risk to life. They occurred about Rough Hey Wood, Triangle, and in the vicinity of Scarr Head Tunnel; and constant removal of masses of earth and rocks, remaking the permanent way and building enormous strengthening walls accounted for the stupendous cost of the line. To protect the tunnel, which was erected in an oval shape and was strongly built with four courses of stone underfoot and six above ground, a retaining wall 87 feet high—one stretch of nearly 500 feet being 26 feet thick—was built to prevent lateral pressure by landslips. The erection of this wall alone was a gigantic undertaking. But all the difficulties and effort and risks were forgotten on the opening day by the people who gave themselves up to the pleasures of the occasion : dwellers in Ripponden, we read, were " delirious with joy at having at last the trains at their doorsteps." When the first passenger train, which left Sowerby Bridge at 8 a.m., arrived in the new gaily decorated station at Ripponden they fired a cannon, set their church bells ringing, took a holiday from work, and the inns held " open house."

This train had a first, a second and three third-class carriages, the fares being 7d., 5d. and 3½d. The Ripponden Brass Band, which had played it in, was sent back on the train to Sowerby Bridge to play lively airs in the town, until it returned on the 2-30 train, which had seven crowded carriages. On that first day 2,000 passengers travelled on the line, " without a single accident "—more than on any other branch line on an opening day, it was officially stated. The line had been opened for goods traffic the previous month.

33

The Roller-skating Rinks.

WHEN the roller-skating craze swept the country about 1874, Halifax was very cautious about constructing a rink—lest, it was suggested publicly, roller-skating might be a passing fashion bringing only fleeting success to the costly rinks being erected elsewhere, with ruin following when the craze vanished. But people followed the rinks, and local demand won the day. At last, on August 19, 1876, the Skating Rink in Arden Road opened with a flourish of bunting and with the West Yorks Artillery Band playing selections. It was a good rink, partly covered, partly open, with a skating surface of over 2,300 square yards, constructed of one-inch thick rock asphalt with a particularly smooth surface. It was declared one of the largest and best, and its floor " could stand competition with any in the country." There was a colonnade for spectators, a retiring-room for ladies, and dressing-rooms. Skates could be hired for sixpence.

On the opening day 200 visitors assembled, most of them putting on skates, and they enjoyed themselves until dark. The Rink became very popular, in the morninsg as a rendezvous for the leisured, the after-noon and evening sixpenny sessions proving great attractions to the general public, skaters and promenaders alike. Exciting events were held from time to time. A " Grand Assault at Arms," for instance, a military display held on December 12, 1883, provided many dramatic items. A detachment of ten men from the 5th Dragoon Guards under their fencing instructor gave demonstrations of fencing. sword and cutlass exercise. They displayed drilling with rapier versus dagger, sword versus cutlass, lance versus sword, sword versus bayonet, and other exploits, concluding with "A Grand Fight for the Cockade." The Rink lent itself perfectly to military uses, and with only brief periods for other purposes it has since been occupied as barracks or headquarters of Service units, as it is to-day.

In 1907 a second wave of roller-skating popularity resulted in the erection of a long, narrow wooden building near Clare Hall (on a site now occupied by part of Trinity Garage) known as the American Skating Rink. It was opened on April 27 in that year. Skating contests and carnivals were held here, too; and there is a report of " the reprehensible behaviour of hooligans " whose sport it was to cause skaters to fall by throwing obstructions in their path from the promenade! In 1908 Sowerby Bridge opened its "Jubilee Cafe and Rink," which survived as a roller-skating rink for about three years.

The statue of Colonel Akroyd.

THE ringing of church bells and the tumultuous cheering of a crowd of 10,000 people that stretched along Northgate and over North Bridge to New Bank, at 3 p.m. on July 29, 1876, proclaimed an event for which Halifax had long been preparing. At noon, the chief citizens of the town had assembled at Bankfield to present an address to Colonel Akroyd, with a testimony that bore 11,757 signatures of Halifax well-wishers. For down at the far end end of the bridge the 10½ft.-high marble pedestal now bore the bronze statue for which it had been waiting some time, and this was the day of the unveiling. The Colonel—like Sir Francis Crossley, 13 years earlier, at the unveiling of his statue in the People's Park—was to be present to receive this honour from the townspeople. And 2,000 workpeople from the Akroyd mills had taken part in a great procession to the statue.

The sculptor, Mr. J. Birnie Philips, had created his 9ft. statue in an excellent likeness of Col. Akroyd in the " easy attitude he frequently adopted when addressing public meetings," it was agreed. Mr. Philips himself had died during the progress of the modelling, and the monument was completed by an Italian colleague from Carrara, being finally cast in bronze in Chelsea. The pedestal bears remarkable historical panels depicting many figures of local prominence, whose features remain very distinct and lifelike in spite of their 80 years' exposure. One of these bronze plaques illustrates the occasion of the cutting of the first sod of the Leeds, Bradford and Halifax Railway on October 20, 1846, the seven figures " in relief " including Col. Akroyd and his father, Mr. Jonathan Akroyd, and the engineer of the new railway. Another depicts the ceremony of the cornerstone-laying of All Souls' Church on April 25, 1856, Sir Gilbert Scott, the architect of the church, and Archdeacon Musgrave being included in the eight figures shown. The Volunteers movement, in the formation of which Col. Akroyd was the prime mover, is commemorated on a third panel in great detail. The remaining plaque bears the Akroyd family coat-of-arms.

In 1901, the statue was removed from North Bridge to its present resting place in the grounds of All Souls' Church, itself one of Col. Akroyd's erections. The trams required the road space at North Bridge, as they had at the other end of the town, when the Prince Consort statue had to be removed from Horton Street to its present position in the same year.

When the artillery range was opened.

THE gun was ready to fire twenty rounds of 32-pounders across Ogden Reservoir, at a target 1,300 yards distant. But the weather, for the third successive day, was "foul and shocking" on that afternoon of September 27, 1875, and the spectators waited for hours exposed to the fury of the wind and the rain for the firing of the first round that was to open the artillery practice range. The firing party of the Halifax Batteries of the 8th West Yorks Artillery left Halifax by omnibus at one o'clock and arrived at the gunsite at two. The opening was timed for three o'clock. But the hundreds of drenched spectators were still doomed to wait. For the colonel had to travel from York, and he was unfortunate in arriving in Leeds just as the Halifax train was leaving. He did not reach Ogden until four-thirty.

Precautions were taken for the safety of unwary people who might be in the danger zone: outposts with flags were stationed on two hill summits to right and left of the firing range. Red flags were to be hoisted on the staffs when firing was to begin.

Use of the range site had been granted by Sir Henry Edwards, Bart., of Pye Nest, and to avoid needless disturbance of game on his moors the outposts were limited to two men each, who were to be in uniform so that they might be recognisable by gamekeepers. Each artilleryman in these look-out positions had to have on him a copy of the regulations controlling the range. Emphasis was placed on *likely disturbance of game by the troops.* How the birds reacted to the deafening noise of the gun's discharge and shrieking through the air of the shells is not reported.

From the moment Miss Holroyd, the daughter of the commanding officer, pulled the lanyard that fired the first round all went well, except the weather. Some of the twenty rounds fell short, others overshot the target and some went wide. But the occasion, in spite of the atrocious conditions, was pronounced a great success, and it was certainly unique in Halifax. The batteries which had the use of this excellent practice range so near to their home station were the envy of other artillery units not so fortunate, the site being declared to be "second to none in the country."

Gunpowder " Plots "

THE chosen spot on the side of Beacon Hill ensured, at least, that one bonfire on November 5, 1874, should be seen by many who could not share directly in the excitement. Its preparation had proceeded according to pattern—but there was something about this " plot " that was to make it more spectacular than anyone but the boys whose private effort it was would expect. For they had taken possession of one of the old cannons the Crimean War and the Indian Mutiny had left distributed about our countryside, trophies of victory brought home as tanks and other war machines were brought as relics from later wars.

The youths hauled the cannon to the scene of their " plot." Into it they rammed a heavy charge of gunpowder—emulating, it may be supposed, the older generation that had come home with stories of the wars—and they followed this by packing brimstone into its muzzle, upending the piece so that its contents could be rammed down hard. Anticipation drove all sense of danger of their operation from the heads of the excited youths and youngsters collected round it.

Without warning the cannon suddenly exploded, giving the boys no chance of escaping from the bursting charge. Miraculously there were no fatal results, although all but one of the fourteen boys present suffered injuries, more or less serious, to their hands and faces. Eleven of the injured were taken from the scene of the accident to the Infirmary, the other two being removed there for treatment the next day. With the unhappy exception of one whose injured hand had to be amputated, all recovered from their wounds. The disastrous results of this " plot " served as warning against the unskilled use of firearms and explosives that was becoming too prevalent.

A grim case of the misuse of gunpowder in this district when it could be procured by all and sundry had been recorded in 1865. To track an unknown thief of coal continually disappearing from his household heap, but " not wishing to cause unpleasantness," its outraged owner inserted some gunpowder in a hole drilled in a good-sized " coblin " of coal, and carefully sealed it. He replaced the coal in a strategic position, " ready for its work," marked it for his own protection and awaited results.

Sure enough the prepared coal had vanished before morning, and during the day a terrible " unaccountable " explosion occurred in a nearby house. The oven was blown from its place, burning coals were scattered, and, we are told, "the nerves of the coal collector received a severe shock." But his coal-thieving activities ceased—and his neighbour was satisfied!

Petition against the Barracks.

IN 1873 reports were circulating in the town that Halifax was to become a permanent military centre—and the worst fears of those opposed to any such idea were aroused. The quartering of troops in barracks or in camp could have nothing but demoralising results, said the opposition, who were not prepared to watch this happen in the town without a fight. A petition for presentation to the Secretary of State for War was circulated for signatures. This prompted other factions in favour of the project of a military barracks to produce rival petitions, and the question became very contentious.

A strong deputation from the borough, armed with the final memorial containing 4,660 signatures, went to London on March 26, 1873, to wait upon H.R.H. the Duke of Cambridge, the Commander-in-Chief, and the Secretary for War, Mr. Cardwell, at the War Office. First, however, our ten representatives obtained an interview with the President of the Local Government Board in Whitehall, Mr. Stansfeld (so respected and well-known in Halifax) and he and a Gen. McDougall accompanied them to the War Office. The objections of " the greater part of the inhabitants," the memorial indicated, were based on the anticipation that immorality would become rife if large bodies of troops were stationed in the town. The deputation informed the War Secretary, who with the C.-in-C. appears to have borne very patiently with them, that " it was the opinion of the inhabitants that such military depots should be established only at a considerable distance from the great centres of population, especially the ones engaged in manufacturing and industrial pursuits, the temptation of frequent parades, reviews and other military spectacles offering strong inducements to neglect of work."

The militia had appeared in Halifax at times, and had been billeted in the public-houses—and the consequences of this practice were responsible for the apprehension in the town. This the deputation pointed out, and the Duke addressed them at some length on this aspect. He said that the depot accommodation would obviate all such billeting and its " attendant irregularities," and assured them that those attached to the depot would be the very best type of soldier and N.C.O., who would have the duties of training recruits.

One week later, visiting bands from Yorkshire cavalry, artillery and rifle regiments were parading the streets, playing lively airs. Good news for the regiments had been confirmed from York, and they were heralding the establishment of the Wellesley Barracks at Highroad Well, which were inaugurated in 1877.

The Church foundation stone fell.

REFERENCES are often made to the existence of a church since 1529 at Lightcliffe, near the site of the historic church erected in 1775, which is still standing but is used only for burial services. When the present St. Matthew's Church was being built to replace it in 1873 a most unusual accident happened during the stone-laying ceremony. A travelling crane had lifted the heavy stone and the place in which it was to rest was prepared in readiness to receive it. The ceremony was attended by many people on a specially erected platform and by some six hundred other spectators.

While the suspended stone was being brought round into position the crane suddenly swung in a wide sweep over the platform, some cast-iron supports having snapped and rendered the whole contraption uncontrollable. There was no means of averting the catastrophe. The large stone crashed down on one end of the crowded platform before anybody could escape. A number of people had limbs broken; several others were crushed or injured in the rush from the platform. Doctors were soon on the scene and a neighbouring house was transformed into a temporary hospital; injured were also looked after in other nearby homes. There were no fatal cases, fortunately. Another crane on the site was brought into action, the stone was raised again, and it was successfully lowered into the place it has occupied for eighty years. The crane, an old wheeled travelling type, was found to have been faulty in a number of places when it was examined to discover the cause of the catastrophe.

Two years later a much happier ceremony took place, when the church was consecrated by the Bishop of Ripon. While the organ, the pulpit, the bells and other necessary and costly items were provided by the people, the church itself had been erected at the cost and generosity of Major Foster, whose wife was holding the trowel in readiness to perform the ceremony at the time the foundation stone had crashed down, and who carried out the formality later.

It is interesting to recall that in the old church the original hand-blown bellows organ is still installed and is in working order after 180 years.

Birthday celebration at Lightcliffe.

MANY occasions are recorded when on one pretext or another banquets or entertainments on a lavish scale were provided. The banquets for Royalty and other distinguished visitors, and dinners and luncheons at local functions, were often of "gargantuan proportions." Eighty or a hundred years ago local employers with hundreds—and in some cases thousands—of men and women working in their mills often entertained them when occasion for celebration arose. One such event of a rather exceptional kind took place on September 20, 1873, in the grounds of a Lightcliffe estate.

This feast was given by Sir Titus Salt at Crow Nest to celebrate his 70th birthday. Special trains from Saltaire brought 4,200 work-people and guests and there on long tables in the gardens were spread lavish provisions. While the railway outing, the relaxation for a few hours in the grounds with the recently erected grotto and waterfall and the enormous conservatories, were part of the celebration, the feast was the special feature, and it was a memorable one. More than a ton of beef, almost a ton of ham, 500 pounds of tongue and 140 pounds of pork pies were disposed of by the visitors; and so were 11,500 buns (currant, seed and plain), 4,500 tarts, 125 stones of bread, 200 pounds of biscuits and 100 stones of apples. Sixty gallons of milk and nearly 900 pounds of sugar were required with the 140 pounds of tea consumed. The event took place during Sir Titus Salt's second period of residence at Crow Nest, only three years before his death. He had lived there from 1844 to 1858, renting the estate from Miss Ann Walker, before going to Methley Park, but he purchased and returned to Crow Nest in 1867. On his 53rd birthday, during his earlier occupation, he had entertained more than 3,000 workpeople from Saltaire Mills on a similarly generous scale, special trains transporting his guests to Bradford and thence to Lightcliffe.

A remarkable enterprise 180 years ago, undertaken by Miss Walker's grandfather, should be recalled in connection with Crow Nest. In 1775, when he was 27, Mr. William Walker went to Hull, chartered a vessel in which he travelled to the eastern Baltic—to buy timber in Russia to be used in the rebuilding of Crow Nest and Cliffe Hill and of the Old Church in Lightcliffe. Returning safely with his cargo he had the timber brought by canal to Brighouse, and from there by wagons to the halls. Before Miss Walker's death in 1856 the Walker family had owned the Crow Nest estate for almost two hundred years.

Wellington Mill Gas Explosion.

THE most rapidly destructive of many Halifax mill fires on record occurred at Messrs. Lister's Wellington Mills, in Lower Wade Street, on December 4, 1873. At earlier big mill fires—Akroyd's Bowling Dyke Mills in 1847 and Whitworth's Lee Bridge Mills in 1853 were instances —only hand-worked engines were there to cope with the conflagrations, and great destruction of property resulted. Improved appliances had been devised by 1873, but they could do nothing to prevent destruction of this six-storey silk mill; they were employed on preventing the fire spreading to the rest of the block of mills, where 600 people were working.

In the lowest storey repairs to a defective meter that supplied 300 gas lights were in hand, and the main pipe had been plugged. The mill was at full work, 120 men, women and children being on the premises. Pressure of gas from the nearby gasworks forced out the plug, for the gas had not been turned off as it was lighting the mill. The lowest floor filled rapidly with gas : the nearest lighted lamp caused the inevitable explosion. There was a blinding flash, and instantly the whole mill was ablaze. The force of the explosion shook the neighbourhood, it was stated. A man blown down in the street reported seeing the bottom storey a mass of flame before he had stood up.

Inside, alarm spread to all floors. Most of the workpeople escaped by a third-floor covered gangway across to another mill in the block. But escape from the upper floors was difficult, for smoke and flame were spreading up the stairways. There were injuries to people who jumped from the windows, burned faces and hands for others who escaped by the stairs and the gangway. Ladders were rushed to the scene and many of the children who had not escaped were rescued by firemen, police and other people. The injured were taken to the Infirmary in cabs.

The fire brigade was joined by a steam fire engine from Dean Clough Mills, and soon eight jets were each pouring about 8,000 gallons of water an hour in efforts to save the other mills. The gangway caught fire, but by a supreme concentration of jets was saved until it was no longer useful for escape. Of the whole " new mill," so-called, only a section of gable wall was left standing.

The tragedy of this fire was the loss of life—five girls, aged eight, eleven, thirteen, fourteen and eighteen, were victims. They were interred at Stoney Royd Cemetery.

Odd Fellows' Hall Mishap.

WHEN on a Saturday evening in November, 1872, a rumour spread through Halifax that a main floor at the Odd Fellows' Hall had collapsed great alarm was caused, and many people rushed to the hall in their anxiety concerning children or friends known to be there. For it was one of the most popular places of entertainment in the town at that time, lively variety shows attracting crowded houses every night. It was not unusual for hundreds to be turned away. Concerts, lectures and public gatherings were also held there. On this evening about a hundred youths, eager to secure front seats, had found their way into the lobby before the doors were officially opened—apparently a common occurrence in spite of precautions against it! At 6-15 the doors opened to admit hundreds more people into the vestibule, where at the foot of the grand staircase the ticket office stood.

Suddenly the floor of the crowded lobby gave way, and the mass of people on it were flung into the rooms below—the ticket-office with the moneytaker disappearing with them. Scenes of wildest confusion followed, it was reported. Cries of those who had fallen and fears and excitement of those above were " past description." The calamity had happened so suddenly that panic seized those left in the lobby. Prompt rescue measures were taken and, fortunately, when medical assistance arrived it was found that of fifty to a hundred people who fell through the five-yard-square aperture only eleven were injured. Eight of these were taken home, the other three to the Infirmary. True to theatrical tradition the show had to go on, and when the victims had been rescued the public were admitted by another door and the performance proceeded. Some basement alterations had entailed partial removal of supporting walls, but the main cause of the catastrophe was found to be a decayed main beam under the vestibule floor. By Monday evening the damaged floor had been repaired and a certificate of safety issued. Another variety company was performing that week, and the mishap did not affect the large nightly audiences.

In March the following year another show—which included the Christy Minstrels—was interrupted by the drop scene suddenly bursting into flames. There was a crowded audience, and scores of people rushed for the doors. But again the show went on, and no damage was suffered except to the drop scene.

The Odd Fellows' Hall Restaurant and Luncheon Bar at that time provided a hot dinner of soup, fish, joint, pudding and cheese for one and sixpence.

Visits of Oriental Ambassadors.

MANUFACTURERS' efforts to expand trade with the Far East in the late 19th century provided colourful diversions for Halifax people. The arrival of envoys of the King of Burma and the Emperor of China respectively, to acquaint themselves with our manufactures and products, were two such occasions. The Burmese Ambassador, with two native secretaries, came by special "handsome saloon carriage" attached to the train from Bradford on September 4, 1872, and were met by the mayoral party and business representatives, at whose invitation their visit was made. Hundreds of people had assembled to see them, and the Chief Constable, mounted, and many police, we learn, kept the crowd in good order. Wearing gorgeous Oriental apparel, "robes of silk of various colours, over which were snowy white tunics," and coronets of feathers above which their hair was plaited into a knot, the distinguished visitors entered the carriages drawn up outside the station. The Mace Bearer accompanied the Mayor, who wore his chain of office. To surmount the language difficulty, a British major who spoke Burmese and a native of Burma who had lived in England many years acted as interpreters.

The Embassy party drove up Horton Street and through the town to Dean Clough Mills for their first tour of inspection. This was followed by a visit to Brunswick Mills. Then the visitors were shown over the Crossley and Porter Orphanage, which greatly impressed them. They saw the assembling of the children for their mid-day dinner, and were photographed on the terrace. Shaw Lodge Mills were next toured, after which the visitors were entertained to luncheon at Manor Heath. Here the president of the Chamber of Commerce presented a message to the Ambassador for his King, respecting trade between this locality and Burma, and requesting the opening up of a projected trade route from Rangoon to facilitate trading with Western China, for which there were " unlimited possibilities."

The Chinese Ambassador's visit was in November, 1899, at the invitation of the Chamber of Commerce. Although he arrived from London late at night, with two Chinese secretaries, several hundred people were at the station and saw the party escorted to the White Swan Hotel. A full day visiting mills and works was spent. His Excellency and his attendants were in Oriental dress, and it was reported that copious notes were made by the secretaries during the tour. In the evening there was a banquet at Bankfield. Many speeches touching on trade between the two countries followed the president's toast : " Prosperity to the Chinese Empire."

Lilly Lane dam burst.

THE bursting of one of the two dams at Lilly Lane Mill in 1872 caused much havoc in what was then a populous part of Halifax. It happened in the dark and consequently was much more alarming; fortunately the last of the workpeople had left the mill. The factory was occupied by Messrs. Marsden Brothers, silk spinners, and other firms, and stood between Lilly Lane and the South Parade Chapel burial ground (cleared in 1883) on the slope above the railway. The dam that burst was only thirty years old and was some twelve yards square with about six feet depth of water; it was at the upper side of the mill, where a new shed was at the time being erected. The collapse of the six-feet-thick embankment was due to the foundations of the new mill extension undermining it. Four or five yards near one corner gave way suddenly at 6 p.m. on November 11.

Water escaped with a tremendous roar, bursting through the mill basement windows with quantities of stones and earth. But this was only the beginning. More water rushed round the side of the mill and devastation was left in its wake. The ground was ploughed up. Gas pipes were burst open as a wall of water and debris swept down Lilly Lane, damaging other premises and flooding many of the small houses and cellar dwellings to a depth of several feet. The warm, dirty water charged with mud and rubbish, had a " pestilential smell," it was reported, which escaping gas did not improve. The steam at first led to a belief that the mill boiler had burst, memories of the terrible explosion at the same mill twenty-two years previously being keen enough to arouse great foreboding until they were dispelled. Ten people had been killed and many injured in that calamity.

The railway viaduct arches just below were used as store-places, and three of these were flooded by one of the streams of rushing water, the large stock of silk within being damaged. At the Bath Tavern at the bottom of Lilly Lane the main flood swept in at the side door, to the sudden alarm of the many occupants, and passed through to escape at the back whence it poured in cascades through holes it forced in an impeding wall down on to the railway. It emptied itself finally into the Hebble near the Bath Parade bridge.

44

They stoned the artist.

A FAMOUS Royal Academician of last century, Mr. H. Stacey Marks, was engaged for the artistic decoration of All Souls' and All Saints' churches, Halifax. During his sojourn here he had some experiences from which he derived amusement in later recollection. In his " Pen and Pencil Sketches " he relates an incident near Salterhebble that had its alarming side. He had left All Saints' one evening after working on the chancel arch, and his eye being attracted by a rugged bit of landscape embracing the nearby mills, he stopped to make some notes and sketches. While he was thus engaged workpeople streaming from the mill added realism to the scene.

But the millhands saw him with pencil and book in his hands looking in their direction—and realism took a very unexpected turn. Mr. Marks concludes from their behaviour that they took him to be " an objectionable overseer." For he recalls the cry that rang out : " 'E's takkin' thi time lads !" Immediately stones were shied at him from the home-going workers " with such precision and rapidity," he says, that, remembering the old proverb about valour and discretion, and failing to appreciate then the humour of the situation, he thought it best to escape from the " playful Yorkshire roughs,"and he beat a hasty retreat. The artist tells us that with the colleague engaged with him at All Souls' Church he used to dine at mid-day in a tavern near the church, where the " ordinary " was partaken chiefly by commercials, and, on market days, " by gigantic farmers with appetites of wonderful enormity " :and he was much entertained by the dexterity with which these diners transferred the gravy from the great dish to their cavernous mouths with their knives !

It was while the two artists were engaged on the mural painting and other decoration at All Souls' Church that they had a memorable experience of local hospitality. They were invited one Sunday to a home a short railway ride from the town, and there they shared the family's mid-day board. A substantial dinner was scarcely swallowed, we are told, before the table was laid again with a heavy tea at which they had to gorge beyond repletion so as not to grieve and hurt their hosts and hostesses. " Huge hams, prodigious joints, eggs poached and boiled, tea cakes hot and buttered, washed down with copious draughts of tea, ensured present distention and future indigestion." And it was with difficulty that they managed afterwards " to waddle rather than walk, like turkeys crammed for Christmas," to the station.

A Merry Christmas.

NEVER can the Christmas weather have been more " unexpectedly perfect " than that which Halifax enjoyed in 1869. It pleased everybody, we read, and added to the festive season's joys. After continuous rain until the 24th the sky cleared, the sun shone brilliantly, and frosty dry air changed the Christmas Eve scene. Light snow fell in the evening, heavy snow on Christmas Day, and sleighs and skates were out in force on Boxing Day. Like Christmas in 1954, this was a three-day festival, all shops and works being closed, and the celebration was acclaimed for this reason as well as for its unsurpassed weather. Not until the 30th did the weather " resume its usual wet and miserable aspect."

At that time the Yorkshire Yeomanry Cavalry regiments quartered here were enlivening the town, trooping in sections about the streets, lending colour and excitement to the everyday scene. When they had first arrived it was reported that they infused life and spirit into Halifax. They would clatter along old Southgate to the Riding School at Ward's End, to be put through their paces with their mounts by the riding masters. Other mounted regiments received training in horsemanship in the arena of the Cavalry Drill Hall, as the Riding School was sometimes called. This was then at the edge of the town. Back through the narrow streets the troops of horse would clatter with a commotion that may be imagined.

At that 1869 Christmas the 2nd West Yorkshire Yeomanry excelled themselves by the ball they gave in the New Assembly Rooms. The company, said the " Guardian " reporter, was a most select one and the ballroom presented a very gay and festive appearance. The colonel of the regiment, Sir Henry Edwards, brought with him Lady Edwards and thirty guests from his mansion at Pye Nest, and there were visiting officers from regiments of Dragoons, Hussars, the Militia and other Yeomanry with their guests. A special quadrille band augmented the regimental band, and the ball was kept going with great animation until five o'clock in the morning. Refreshments and liquor were on a scale in keeping with the occasion.

Half a ton of plum pudding was provided for the Christmas dinner in the workhouse, and with the 300 pounds of roast beef from prize bullocks, 50 gallons of beer, 20 gallons of rum sauce and two cartloads of potatoes made the meal for the participants a memorable one. There were apples and oranges for everyone, tobacco and snuff for adults, and " spice in lieu of beer " for the children. Plum cake in large quantities was consumed at teatime on Boxing Day.

46

Four men in a boat.

IF the idea of a midnight cruise on the River Calder had occurred to
the quartet when they were sober they would at least have selected
a more salubrious stretch of the river than that between the weirs in the
heart of Sowerby Bridge mill-land.   But after a jolly evening at a public-
house, from which the four emerged merrily on that midsummer's night
in 1872, they were not selective in their target for the night.   They had
acquired a spare bottle of whisky, and it could not be taken to four
different homes : this was sufficient reason for their commandeering a
boat they espied moored outside the Moulder's Arms.

Before launching out into mid-stream, however, the absence of oars
in the boat presented a serious problem.   To set this to rights one
scrambled ashore again, procured part of somebody's hen-roost, and
returned on board.   With this as a means of propulsion the boat was
borne up-river; and eventually the cruisers docked their craft in the
" goit " at Hollings Mill.   There, it seems, the spirits were poured down
to keep their spirits up, and the inevitable moment arrived when one
of the jovial party, " noted for vocal power," mounted a seat to sing
to his comrades.

This was asking for trouble, and he had hardly begun when he fell
headlong into the water.   Amid much commotion he was pulled aboard,
having suffered no loss but his hat.   Later, there was another immersion
when one of the others insisted on landing, for the boat during the
confusion was pushed off-shore, and the deserter stepped into the river.
This caused great hilarity, but his companions managed to rescue him,
too.   It was 3 a.m. when this cruise ended and the four men, wet and
sobered, abandoned their boat and sought their ways homeward.

If a boat was a strange night target a stranger was a newly dug
grave that was the choice of a Halifax gravedigger in October, 1844.
From the Ring o' Bells, on being refused further refreshment, he crossed
to the churchyard and wandered among the familiar tombstones.
Presently, undressing in the apparent belief that he had reached home,
he lay down and slept in the product of his day's handiwork.   He was
found in the grave by searchers, and there was much shouting before
the sleeper was roused to the realisation that he was not in his own bed !

Lively opening for North Bridge.

FOR almost 100 years the narrow six-arch stone bridge across the Hebble had carried the wagons and the coaches to and from Halifax, having itself replaced a wooden predecessor in 1770. But in 1871 the new iron two-span North Bridge, 60 feet wide, was opened with due ceremony and demonstration. The procession, in spite of its imposing nature, " fell short of what the occasion required," according to a reporting spectator; but sensation enough was provided by the lined-up wagons at the New Bank entrance barrier before the opening, their drivers eager to be the first to cross. Foremost was a wagon piled high with wool, as a staple commodity of Halifax, drawn by four gaily decorated horses.

The trouble was that this wagon-load completely blocked the view of the thousands of people watching in Range Bank and on the nearby slopes, and the resulting uproar compelled it to draw back into Haley Hill. Here was the chance for a lorry in Charlestown Road, which at once slipped into the vacant front rank, stealing priority. The wool wagoners were not going to stand for this, and they moved their mountainous vehicle back to the barrier, contriving to force the interloper from the first place. Immediately another lorry drew alongside the latter, and the two drivers, disputing for second place, entered the bridge side by side behind the wool wagon instead of in file. Reporters observed that it was a miracle that only one serious casualty occurred, as these projecting second-place vehicles forced back the crowd lining the bridge near the official and ladies' platforms, and it had to be warned by cries to make more room.

There were other disturbances that must have helped to make the occasion memorable to those officially taking part. The two 32-pounder guns in Southowram Road, which were to have heralded the opening, fired out of turn, during the prayer and the speeches preceding the formal opening. The bells of All Souls' and the Parish Church, signalled thus by the guns, added their acclamations before they were due, and " somewhat marred " (said one reporter) the preliminaries. No doubt they enlivened the ceremony for the crowds. There was the release of a Montgolfier balloon to give wider publicity to the opening; and a banquet later for the officials and distinguished guests. And so North Bridge —a masterpiece of foresight adequate for traffic nearly a century later, although declared at the time to be the cheapest bridge in the country at 17s. 6d. per square foot of roadway—was happily inaugurated and became the new artery it is to-day.

48

The Wainhouse Tower.

|F Mr. J. E. Wainhouse and Sir Henry Edwards, enemies in their private
wars eighty years ago, could by some magic have been together on a
highway leading to Halifax on one of the Coronation nights in 1953,
they surely would have marvelled at the apparition high in the sky that
met their eyes—at the spectacle of beauty at the top of the Tower, that
contentious erection that was the pride of one and the bane of the other.
The electricians had performed a miracle, displaying by their lights the
16 stately pillars on the first platform and the graceful ornamental
stonework crowning the column 250 feet up. Any old enmity must
have been forgotten as the two incredulous observers came closer, and
from the nearby roadway took in the full illumined splendour of the
tracery in stone, so delicate but so massive, revealed by the lights as it
had never been by the sun. Incredible that this was the outcome of
that original dispute about Smoke!

And what of the Tower itself. from its beginnings in 1870, the
chimney to carry away the dyeworks' smoke about which Sir Henry and
the Smoke Abatement Society had so long complained and pestered Mr.
Wainhouse? Of the promise to cease complaints and suspend the summons while the chimney was being erected; the continual persecution in
spite of this undertaking that led Mr. Wainhouse to his crowning act of
retaliation—the encasing of his chimney in two feet of stone, the lavish
ornamentation at the summit so perfectly and solidly completed. the
construction of the 400 steps up the seven-foot flue to the platform from
which the world around, including Sir Henry's Pye Nest mansion, could
be viewed by anybody? How gratifying the exasperation of the enemies
at being so subtly tricked! A strange story of a strange revenge, that
cost its perpetrator £10,000, it was declared.

" Wainhouse Folly," " Octagon Tower "—whatever name was applied in derision or, later, in appreciation—the monument remained as a
landmark of Halifax when its creator died in 1883. It was sold, and sold
again. It was advertised in 1887 as an attraction : " Octagon Tower.
Open for admission every Saturday afternoon, if fine; admission 2d.."
It was offered for sale by auction in 1912. In 1918 it was acquired by
a shilling fund run by the " Halifax Courier " and handed to the Corporation. It was used experimentally for wireless telegraphy forty years
ago. In a storm it was struck by lightning, and nine feet of the stonework was blown from the top. But it was repaired, and the Tower was
there at the threat of war to serve as an observation post; is there to play
its part as an illuminated adornment on great occasions, and remains a
curious but unique feature of Halifax for all who see to wonder at.

" Sales-talk " of last century.

IF you had been uncertain whether to buy a fire engine you saw
advertised as " a bargain " in the daily sales column of the " Halifax
Courier " in 1869, you might have had your mind made up for you
by the offer of a free demonstration—provided you did not expect the
engine to be brought into action quickly. For it could only be seen
working on giving two days' notice. It was described as one of the
best engines in Yorkshire, had seven pumps, and its piping could be
bought or left, as desired. If you were not convinced by all this that
you really needed a fire engine, there were other attractive offers in the
local Press, no matter when the problem of buying a present for somebody or for yourself arose.

A cartload of snow, for instance, could be bought for three shillings
if you rode over to Hebden Bridge and were interested in the sample
load deposited outside the " Hole-in-the-Wall Inn." This snow was of
a hard, crystalline nature, you would be informed, and it was declared
by the local character who brought it down from Wadsworth Moor that
morning in May, 1844, to have lain out there for three months. And
he guaranteed to supply any orders up to 50 tons of this snow any day
until the end of June! But it seems that this snow-seller's unique trading
offer was thwarted by nature taking a hand in the business : his commodity
ceased to have a scarcity value, for in that same May week snow fell to
such an extent that the hillsides were covered again—and stayed so far
into the summer!

If, say, in 1866, you had felt like having your washing done for you,
you could have taken it across to Haley Hill, where a new invention
advertised in the " Courier " would have washed, dried and mangled it
for you the same day. The advertiser, Mr. Coton, informed the public
that he had opened a public washhouse fitted up with patent machinery
for washing and drying by steam power all kinds of bed linen and
bedding, blankets, etc., and that hotel keepers and others having large
washings would find this a rare opportunity. "All parties desirous to
see washing without knuckles, and with the least possible violence to
the fabric," were invited to call on the days appointed.

It might be said, in fairness to the past, that our " modern " laun-
derettes, like our pocket-lighters, are not quite so modern as we had
thought. Those " portable pocket gaslighters " were advertised by a
Halifax shopkeeper a century and a half ago.

The crowded pavement gave way.

THE elevated pavement outside the Old King Cross Inn made a grand-stand for the autumn "Rushbearing" festivities that were held with great enthusiasm at King Cross. The streets were the scenes of the donkey races, the pole-climbing exploits and other sporty features There were hustlers' carts and fair stalls for the sale of toys, and of course "daring and ambitious youth," stripped to the waist, all had to duck their heads into the tub of water, "bobbing" for the floating apples. But the donkey racing was a highlight of the September, 1867, celebrations—or would have been had not a most unexpected mishap occurred in the early evening when the race was about to start.

An iron palisade 25 yards long lined the edge of the elevated pavement on to which crowded the boys and girls of King Cross who were quick enough to get there first to view the race. Under their pressure the whole length of railing gave way, the children being thrown into the road about four feet below. There was great commotion, and the whole scene changed : there were broken limbs, and other spectators, too, were injured. Criticism was made afterwards that the railing had been insecure for years. Part of this raised pavement is there to-day.

The year before another "fall" on a road had occurred in Halifax. Then it was a wall, not railings, and it happened without any human pressure being the cause. It was nearly 50 feet high and 100 feet long, in North Corporation Street, and had been erected at the joint cost of owners of neighbouring property and the Corporation. The wall had shown cracks and signs of weakening, and precautions to prevent its collapse had been made. It fell on March 4, 1866, with a "loud rumbling noise." As this happened at 4 a.m. it awakened the neighbourhood and caused much alarm, many people rushing into the streets to discover the cause.

North Corporation Street had been constructed to provide a short link between Lee Bridge and the town centre, and it came in for much criticism (and witticism) when it was new and had for some time been left unfinished, one correspondent to the "Halifax Guardian" in 1852, reminding fellow readers that just as North Parade when first made had been nicknamed "Needless," this new street, "given its lofty name by anticipation," should be called "Useless." As Corporation Street, after 100 years in use, its value to the town could more accurately be described as "Priceless."

The new bonding warehouse collapsed.

THE Inland Bonding Warehouse stands solidly there in Gibbet Street, Halifax, appearing dark and rather forbidding to passers-by. But it was not always so solid. The wall of the building erected to replace the old warehouse in Church Street which the trade of the town had outgrown, was almost completed, when on January 28th, 1867, much of the rear part of it was blown down in a gale. The long cellar with its fireproof ceiling that formed the floor of the ground-level storage warehouse, supported on iron pillars, had been finished, and the roof was in process of fixing, when the first collapse happened. And a long section of the rear wall was left dangerously unsupported.

Just before work was resumed at 1 p.m. this wall, too, collapsed, battered by a powerful gust of wind, and with a terrific crash roof timbers, pillar supports and masonry fell with it to the floor—which was the ceiling of the long cellar. The brick arches beneath were unable to withstand the sudden weight and in turn gave way, the whole mass of debris falling through into the cellar. Of the new bonding warehouse only two walls and part of the ground floor remained. It had to be rebuilt; and it was opened on April 25th, 1868.

This early calamity was not the worst to befall the bonding warehouse. There had been no loss of life on its first collapse, by a fortunate chance of timing : in the next there was. The new building had to be enlarged in 1872, and the single undivided cellar, 240 feet long, for cask and barrel storage, with the enlarged ground-level space increased the capacity by nearly one-third. Again brick arches supported on iron pillars carried the ground floor. And during the process of digging round a pillar for the foundation of strengthening brickwork the pillar slipped from its stone base—and with the arch it was supporting it crashed down, bringing a portion of the floor with it.

Two workmen and a Customs and Excise employee were buried under the pile of brickwork and debris. One of the men was almost buried in the hole he had dug, but he was saved by the pillar falling across it. Completely lost to view, it was two hours before he was extricated, badly crushed, and removed to the Infirmary. The other two men were dead when brought out. Barrels and casks had rolled down from the store above. The roof was weakened, and temporary supports had to be erected while rescue work proceeded. Before the repaired structure was re-opened in 1872 every precaution had been taken against future calamity.

Police guard for the auctioneer.

IN the Halifax of 1866 the compulsory vaccination of children was being actively opposed by many of the townspeople, and lively scenes were kept in check only by strong intervention by the police. Much of the trouble resulted from seizure of furniture for non-payment of fines imposed by the Bench on householders who refused to have their children vaccinated. In one instance bailiffs had been in possession of two houses for seven days, because of the refusal to pay fines amounting, with costs, to £1 9s. 6d. in each case. Then the articles were delivered to the fire station, where sales of distrained goods took place.

While the bellman was announcing the sale in the town a furniture wagon bearing a red banner with the words " Halifax Anti-Compulsory Vaccination League. Justice and Freedom! Jenner's Patent Run Out!" paraded the streets. The vicinity of the fire station was crowded long before the sale time—and with the crowd were four plain-clothes detectives, twenty-four policemen under an inspector, with the Chief Constable and the Town Clerk. Other police were drawn up in the engine house, where the furniture was barricaded from the attending crowd.

The auctioneer from Huddersfield mounted the rostrum, announced the conditions and opened the sale. From that moment opposition to him began. One man shouted a demand that he show his licence, and this caused an altercation between the auctioneer and the crowd. There was hissing and booing, and confused bidding was deliberately provoked. But the required sum had to be raised; the auctioneer had to continue. When he demanded immediate cash from one troublesome buyer— the upholder of the A.C.V. League—and was refused, the Town Clerk was appealed to, and he upheld the auctioneer.

There was uproar when instant cash was *not* required from a non-member. But the end came when sufficient articles had been sold to cover the fines and costs. Then the crowd helped the league stalwart, the buyer of all but one lot, to load the furniture on to the wagon, which was draped with the league flag, and they cheered it on its way back to the houses from which it had been seized.

It was some time before the auctioneer could safely leave; and when he did he was escorted by police to the station for his train to Huddersfield.

Nor was the bailiff's lot a happy one. One householder, expecting them, removed the room carpet, the chairs and everything that could provide comfort for the visitors, not forgetting, as it was January, to rake out the fire and to remove the fuel. His family locked itself and its possessions in the upstairs room : they had the best of the seige— while it lasted.

Ten-weeks' Circus at Ward's End.

"A MAGNIFICENT establishment modelled on the Cirque Champs Elysee in Paris," said the announcements of the temporary building erected at Ward's End, Halifax, in March, 1865, for Mr. J. W. Myers's Grand American Circus. And lest it be assumed that this was an exaggeration, the "Halifax Guardian" reporter assured readers that the advertisements did not overrate the building's splendour. Its beauty of architecture was striking and it was ideally adapted for its purpose. The roof was supported by eight pillars surrounding the ring, each adorned by an emblematic figure—Hercules, Bacchus, and others. Paintings illustrative of the four continents and the four seasons decorated the ceiling; 800 gas lights provided "radiant illumination"; the lower-priced seats at sixpence were designed for comfort as were the top-price ones at two shillings. Boxes, which could be reserved, were papered and carpeted, and were lighted by crystal chandeliers. Reports confirmed that the building was draughtproof and rainproof, as claimed. It was "perfumed by Rimmel's patent vapouriser." Local builders erected it to Mr. Myer's' plans.

This circus that was "different" flourished for ten weeks, changing the performance every other evening, introducing new performers each week, and providing two shows on Saturdays. There was a galaxy of performing animals, acrobats, gymnasts, equestrian artistes, gladiators, matadors, contortionists and clowns. There were two performing mules "whose tricks put those of all other performing animals into the shade." Their special attraction derived from the fact that nothing could persuade or drive them to act in any way differently from the part assigned to them; and when members of the audience were invited to ride these "harmless low comedians"—a popular turn with the crowd at each show—they were promptly thrown off. A boy of eleven, styled "The Equestrian Wonder of the World," created a furore, always being repeatedly recalled on his spotted charger.

On Easter Monday and Tuesday two grand fetes and galas were held in the grounds adjoining, at which men and women of the circus performed special feats as additional attractions to the sports, races, the greasy pole, sideshows and two brass bands. These galas were so successful that the event was repeated on the Saturday, and this occasion concluded with a display of fireworks.

A licence for performing stage plays was granted to Mr. Myers for his Hippodrome, for he intended that his building should remain, to be available for a return visit by his circus. At his final performance many prizes and presents were given away—including a horse, won by a resident of Upper Brunswick Street.

An early rail crash at Elland.

" SUCH an enormous amount of passenger and goods train traffic passes between Halifax, North Dean and Elland that the wonder is there are not more accidents.

" Trains follow each other in such rapid succession that it becomes marvellous how signals are made to indicate danger and safety with the regularity they do."

This comment from a report of a collision within four miles of Halifax on November 15, 1865, gives us to-day a picture of the activity of the local line some 20 years after its construction.

An express train left Halifax at 10-30 on the fateful morning for Huddersfield, " non-stop to Brighouse." Immediately before the express an empty coal train moved out from North Dean (Greetland) towards Elland, where it was to shunt on to the up-line to allow the express to pass. The driver of this coal train therefore knew that the Halifax express was to follow.

The driver of the express saw the line was clear when he emerged from the cutting; he put on steam and passed North Dean. His train then entered the tunnel. Before it was through he could see the coal train on the same line, between the end of the tunnel and Elland station. He was running at such a speed that it was impossible to avoid a collision. He slackened speed a little, shutting off steam and reversing the engine. Then he jumped for his life.

The next moment the express crashed into the coal train—with such force that " noise of the terrible crash was heard all over Elland." The engine ploughed through the guard's van of the coal train shivering it to matchwood. Girders and framework were " bent and twisted, torn asunder." Coal wagons shot forward into Elland station, many being smashed to splinters and scattered in all directions.

Meanwhile the express driver had escaped, thanks to his leap from the engine, with only slight injury to his knee. There were only 11 passengers in his train, and though all were injured, miraculously there were no bones broken. A surgeon attended to the casualties in the waiting-room and in the public-house near the station yard.

" Neglect " was found to be the cause of the accident, and the coal train driver was dismissed by the railway company.

Rather acid comment followed the newspaper report : " No doubt there will be a strict inquiry instituted by the railway authorities, but would it not be better if the directors, instead of wasting time after such accidents, took steps to prevent similar ones for the future?"

Tragedy of balloon ascent at Piece Hall.

A MUCH-HERALDED gala, with the sensation of the day the promised "Ascent of a Balloon" from the Piece Hall. The owner of the balloon to make the ascent in its suspended car.

On September 12, 1863, these were reasons enough, without the other alluring attractions such as the performance of a "Fire King," for the vastness of Halifax's Piece Hall to be filled with an expectant, excited crowd that Saturday afternoon. And sensation enough they had before the event was over.

Four hours it took for "The Volunteer," as the balloon was named, to be inflated, but at six o'clock, Mr. Youings, the owner, mounted into the car. He was to have taken a woman passenger, but, fortunately for her in view of what happened, he went aloft alone.

The first check to a successful ascent occurred only a few yards from the ground, when the car caught the telegraph wires which crossed the open space of the Piece Hall. But the dismay at this mishap voiced by the crowd—which was out for excitement, not disappointment—was nothing to what was to follow. Every precaution had been taken, it was believed, to allow for a clear ascent, avoiding the wires, the three-storey wall, the high chimney of Firth & Son's Mill, and the spire of Square Chapel, south-east of the Hall.

Eventually released from the wires without serious damage, "The Volunteer" rose again. As it cleared the wall only by the narrowest margin, the crowd gasped with the suspense, and then they watched it being driven by the westerly wind—directly towards the dreaded obstructions! With shouts and shrieks of horror, the massed spectators saw the rising, swinging car strike the top of the chimney, and stick there. The great envelope above, heaving backwards and forwards in the wind, provided an alarming spectacle.

The crowds rushed forward, filling the mill yard, the yard of the chapel, and the surrounding streets. They saw the balloon burst, and, as the gas rapidly escaped, collapse and fall across the chimney's mouth. The unfortunate Mr. Youings was suspended in his car one hundred and twenty-five feet above the ground with no apparent means of descent. But the crowd saw him take off his hat and wave to them with it, and they yelled in admiration at this gesture. He was a hero.

An hour later, he was still suspended; and it was nearing nightfall. But something was happening up there. He was seen to be paying out a long rope, secured to the hanging car, down the chimney side—a desperate last resort for a descent. Breathlessly the crowd watched him climb out of the car, and slowly, hand over hand, lower himself. The rope was too short, but by means of a long ladder manoeuvred by helpers below, he descended the last few yards—and was carried away to the Talbot Inn to be feted.

The real tragedy was yet to come. All night the balloon was covering the chimney top, and the fires in the mill boiler had to be ready for Monday. While the Sunday morning service in Square Chapel was in progress, a stalwart local steeplejack, by name Rawson, climbed the long rope by which Youings had descended, to attempt to dislodge the heavy, sagging envelope. Arrived near the top, exhausted, he rested— and the rope, chafed or weakened somewhere just above him, snapped. The cries of the crowd were heard in Square Chapel as Rawson fell those hundred and twenty-five feet to his death.

Disaster at Piece Hall gathering.

ON April 7, 1858, two mishaps occurred in the Piece Hall, Halifax, in the first of which many people were injured. The occasion was the visit of the eminent preacher, the Rev. Charles H. Spurgeon. A large timber structure to accommodate 8,000 people had been erected, covering more than 2,500 square yards of the Piece Hall area, a gallery erected on the west side providing 2,000 seats and the other sections the remaining 6,000. Places in the gallery were free, the rest requiring varyingly priced tickets.

In spite of heavy unexpected snow, between 4,000 and 5,000 people attended the afternoon meeting, which, like the later one, had for its object the wiping off of the Trinity Road Baptist Church debt, and a greater number still were present in the evening.

The first accident occurred when the evening congregation was leaving. A portion of the platform of three-inch planks erected along the north-west colonnade, which provided access to and exit from the gallery, collapsed under the pressure of the moving crowd. Thirty or 40 people were thrown down among the falling planks, many being jammed between them. Rescue in some cases was difficult and dangerous. Two people had fractured legs and were taken to the Infirmary. Most of the others suffered minor injuries.

Another disaster was to follow. During the night the entire erection became a shapeless mass of wreckage. The light roof—part of timber and part of tent canvas—gave way under the 150 tons of snow it was estimated had collected on it. With rending crashes it collapsed, smashing all the upright pillars, crushing the forms where the thousands had sat, tearing down gas pipes and doing other extensive damage. The canvas was torn to shreds.

The total damage sustained and the expenses incurred were estimated to require the whole of the money received from the 10,000 people who had occupied the building—leaving nothing to be handed over to the fund for which the occasion had been planned.

State Occasion at the Station.

IT was the first ceremony at which Halifax's Mayor and Corporation appeared in public wearing their new robes of office. This memorable fact was rather overshadowed by the importance of the event itself, the arrival of the Prince of Wales on August 3, 1863, for his two-day visit, on the second of which he opened the new Town Hall. The Corporation officials made a colourful spectacle entirely new to the townspeople, as they progressed to the special raised platform in the station, with other prominent citizens and guests, to await the Royal train.

The Mayor's black robe was trimmed with rich silk velvet, bordered with ermine; he wore the gold chain of office, and his cocked hat. The robes of the aldermen were bright scarlet, the councillors' light purple, while the Town Clerk, also wearing a cocked hat, wore a robe of black. The dignified beadle—then in his 74th year—outshone them all in splendour, we are told. His scarlet waistcoat and his drab coloured coat with bright buttons were trimmed with gold lace, and he wore knee breeches and his large cocked hat. Bearing the mace, he led the Corporation party down to the station platform.

The well-laid plans of the L. and Y. superintendent in charge of the station arrangements went awry through no fault of his. He had marked the position where the engine of the Royal train should stop to ensure that the Prince should descend to the carpeted platform directly opposite the assembled officials. But advices to him of the composition of the train had not included the addition at Wakefield, where engines were changed, of the railway directors' gondola coach immediately behind the new engine. This vehicle was 36 feet long, and the result was that when the train stopped—ten minutes before it was expected, incidentally—the Prince stepped down to the unprepared platform a dozen yards from the waiting Mayor and Corporation. They, taken completely by surprise, had to abandon their dais and hurry along the platform to meet His Royal Highness. This did not add to the dignity of the occasion; and there was much disappointment, for everything but this unforseen occurrence had been allowed for.

A minor hitch occurred outside the station, afterwards. Owing to the premature arrival of the train and the earlier-than-planned state departure of the mayoral carriage bearing the Prince, with the escort of artillery and yeomanry with their bands, the specially made carpet that was to have been laid to the carriage arrived at the station after the procession had moved off for Manor Heath, where the Prince was to be the guest of Mr. John Crossley.

358 Trains for Town Hall opening.

WHEN the Prince of Wales, the future King Edward VII, visited Halifax to open the new Town Hall on August 4, 1863, the Lancashire and Yorkshire Railway rose to the occasion on a prodigious scale. The facts of their achievement here nearly a century ago make astonishing reading to-day. Two hundred and fifty men on duty at Halifax station; 60 extra ticket-collectors at Sowerby Bridge, North Dean (Greetland), Low Moor, Hipperholme and Brighouse; a man placed at every mile distance along the lines from Halifax to Bradford, to Cleckheaton, to Wakefield and to Todmorden with special signals to cope with the streams of trains on all these routes, and others at stations between Huddersfield and Holmfirth; "electric-telegraph" men at all tunnels with orders not to allow two trains through at the same time; platelayers on duty every half-mile in the local area.

Spare engines were in readiness at Sowerby Bridge and at Low Moor to take back incoming trains, to avoid loss of time by changing engines round. Altogether 358 trains were handled at Halifax during the two days' celebrations. Tickets issued from outside stations to Halifax on the "opening" day alone numbered almost 70,000. And all this was in spite of the bride Princess's visit having been cancelled and of the incessant rain reducing the number of visitors. The crowds were looked after in the town by 870 police—200 of them from London, others from Liverpool, Leeds, Sheffield and elsewhere. Detectives "with knowledge of tramping vagabonds who live on plunder" arrived and they arrested 18 persons in the act of picking pockets or as suspicious characters. The "pitiless rain" spoiled the special platform viewing arrangements, and many stands were unused; yet more than 100,000 people witnessed the ceremony or the processions.

Feeding the enormous throngs seems to have produced problems of over-supply, not of shortage. One eating-house was left with 700 loaves, which were sold to clear at a penny each. Another caterer had 30 boiled hams and 60 pounds of beef on his hands when the last customer had been fed.

The enterprise of a certain innkeeper deserves to be recalled. He had erected a stand outside his public-house for the convenience of patrons, but nobody patronised it because of the charge for seats, and the rain. He offered free seats, but this was not sufficient inducement, because there was still rain. So a bonus of a tasty meat sandwich was offered with a free seat. This "took," and the sandwiches being so salty that great thirsts were promoted, a demand for ale resulted which gained for our innkeeper his ultimate reward.

Salmon in the Calder.

" **I** COULD take my rod, or send my keeper, if a friend came unexpectedly to dinner and have a salmon for him to a certainty . . .
The Calder only a few years ago was a brilliant fishing river." These
were passages from a Fishery Inspector's report read in the House of
Commons on March 8, 1865, when a Rivers Pollution Bill was in debate.
And that inspector, having fallen into the Calder, knew his subject!
" There is no salmon in the Calder now," his report complained, " and
so strong is the influence of dyestuff contained in it that, slipping off
the bank last summer, I underwent immersion in the water, and my
Russian duck trousers were dyed a determined blue which defied the
power of bleaching to obliterate." Like a hundred others the river had
become " poisonous."

Immersion in the Calder was by choice in the case of a hawker,
of Elland, commonly known as "Ali Trip." We are told there was no
man in Elland-cum-Greetland in 1860 better known than he " for foolish
acts." This eccentric character had developed a sensational habit of
lying on the parapet of Elland Bridge, informing passers-by that he
intended to drown himself; he would then roll off the edge into the
Calder thirty feet below. Little notice was taken of the announcements
that introduced these strange displays, but the splashes and flounderings
as he came to land were applauded. "Ali" would resume his hawking
in his wet clothes, boasting how cleverly he had saved himself. But
everybody knew he would roll over the parapet again before long, for
these " intended " deaths were life to "Ali Trip."

On this subject of falling, we might recall the two men who in
June, 1864, asked permission to ascend to the balcony of Halifax Town
Hall tower, from which there was a fine view. One was a discharged
soldier who confessed to having been converted at the recent " Revival "
services at the Odd Fellows Hall. They were allowed to go up. Soon
afterwards the constable on duty in the Town Hall thought he heard
singing up aloft, and mounting the staircase he found the two men
lustily singing a revival hymn. One fell to his knees, praying—and the
officer's objection to this behaviour was due to the large crowd he saw
collecting below to gaze up at the tower in astonishment. He ordered
the " Revivalists " to come down, but they refused—until they were
offered the alternative of obeying or of martyrdom by " going over the
railings into the street." They chose the safer descent!

The Empire and an Umpire.

IT took a long time to travel about the Empire ninety years ago, and the promise held out by the Stereopticon at the Mechanics' Hall drew Halifax people in crowds twice a day one week in May, 1863. The optical diorama exhibiting "The World We Inhabit" took the audiences incredible distances in two hours. If you are not clear about the Stereopticon that displayed "Sun Paintings and Sun Sculpture of the most beautiful in Nature and Art"—and who is, in this enlightened age?—you might be more certain about the Stereograph. This was twenty to forty feet in diameter and depicted mountains, lakes, rivers, forests, cathedrals, castles, palaces and the world's architecture and sculpture.

The people in the Mechanics' Hall were shown round the Empire, viewed State apartments in Venice, Rome and Paris, saw the treasures of the Vatican and the Louvre, the Pyramids and other monuments of Egypt—all shown on "200 feet of Illuminated Canvas with Beauty and Perfection never before witnessed." There was, too, a gallery displaying the noblest statuary of ancient and modern times, and a portrait gallery which included authentic portraits of the Prince and Princess of Wales.

These unfamiliar appliances of long ago, the Stereopticon and the Stereograph, were assisted by another, a Stereoscope, which demonstrated the lectures describing all the scenes. For sixpence you could have had the benefit of all this—thirty-five years before Halifax folk saw the first animated pictures!

But you may have been more fond of outdoor sport than of indoor travel, in which case you would have enjoyed seeing Elland supporters at a cricket battle between their team and their Brighouse rivals sweep on to the field and drive the umpire off it, so disapproving were they of that Brighouse gentleman's decisions. Several times, it was reported, owing to the number of batsmen given out "leg before," the crowds "got their danders up" and shouted their disagreement with the honest umpire.

It had been bad enough when the first ball knocked out the Elland "professional" and the third hit the batsman's leg and started the epidemic of leg hits. For a space the game waxed merry while "a heavy batter whisked the ball all around," until, being also hit on the leg, the daring umpire had ordered this hero, too, to "go."

That was too much. The umpire was chased off, escaped to a safe place, and the game was stopped. Brighouse refused to resume although invited. "Wicked folk," we read, "suggested that the Elland committee would not have cared so much had the pies and beer been consumed, for they had expected a pot of money" from this source!

Snapshots about the Town.

THE whirlwind that without warning attacked a hayfield at Norland one Sunday noon in 1863 was a rare phenomenon. It swept the small haycocks from the field and whirled them about at a great height. Some were carried a distance of two miles, coming to earth near Sowerby Church.

An accident occurred the year before to one of Halifax's new gas-holders, 100 feet in diameter. As the ponderous cylinder was being lowered after testing, one side stuck fast in the frame, while the rest of it, unimpeded, continued descending. The whole gasholder over-balanced and collapsed, breaking up in a complete wreck. Fortunately no one was injured.

The arrival on the People's Park lake of a pair of Royal swans aroused much local interest in 1861. They were a gift from Queen Victoria.

A week-end in 1887 was enlivened for Highroad Well by a riot among gipsies encamped on the racecourse. On the Saturday some had been drinking heavily, and had got to fighting among themselves. Dis-order outside their camp brought people flocking to the scene on the Sunday when "hostilities" were resumed. In the general melée one elderly gipsy was badly injured and was taken to the Infirmary, his wife having an arm broken while trying to defend him.

In 1806 a blind youth of 18 set off to run to Leeds; given eight minutes start, he had to beat the mail coach from Halifax, via Clayton Heights and Bradford. He was within four miles of Leeds when the coach overtook him, and he lost the five guineas wager. But he won another by running the 18 miles in under three hours. He was without guide as far as Bradford; from there he had a mounted guide, and he held the running horse's stirrup.

The announcement of a " Popular Lecture for Working People " nearly 100 years ago reads strangely to-day. It was in the Oddfellows Hall, Mr. John Crossley presiding. "Admission: Body of Hall and Gallery, one penny. Reserved Seats, sixpence. Surplus will be given to the Infirmary." The subject was " The Rise, Progress and Present Position of Turkey."

As for the resource of the two youths who, in 1859, had no toll money for a donkey they had to take out of the town, one is filled with admiration. They carried the animal past the toll-bar, his forelegs over the shoulder of the leader, his rear part burdened by the other, we know not how. What the toll-keeper thought privately about the donkey that rode through on four pedestrian feet we shall never know, either. But it was recorded that he complained vocally that he had been cheated.

Mammoth tea and meeting.

THE arrival of 400 more visitors for tea than were expected provided excuse enough for chaos that Saturday afternoon in April, 1863, when the Halifax Flour Society's brand new mill at Bailey Hall was opened. But the enterprising Flour Society rose to the occasion, and though we read that there was the utmost bustle and confusion at the tea to which 1,000 had been invited in celebration of the mill's opening, the 1,400 people who turned up were all fed handsomely.

The meal was in progress for four hours. The prodigious quantity of food in readiness—including five large hams, 150 pounds of beef, 40 pounds of potted meat, 3,000 buns (currant, Bath and plain), 30 stones of bread and 600 teacakes—was augmented from outside sources to satisfy the extra 400 mouths. All the visitors, we learn, were happy and cheerful and enjoyed themselves on that gay and busy opening occasion.

The new six-storey corn mill had been built on the site of the small mill where the society's operations had been conducted since 1847. It now had an up-to-date mill with a 20h.p. engine and grinding machinery comprising fourteen pairs of French stones and two pairs of meal stones with all the newest improvements; silks were to be used for dressing the flour. The upper floors provided space for enormous stores of wheat and flour and other commodities. The mill was declared to be one of the most substantial, commodious and complete corn mills in the country.

While the public meeting in the evening proceeded, diversions and amusements were provided on the floor above for the surplus visitors many of whom " joined in the merry maze of Terpsichore." The string band engaged divided its activities between the dancing and the concert which entertained the meeting below, given by the Glee and Madrigal Society and other soloists. When the band played an overture and received an enthusiastic encore the instrumentalists had to decline and hurry upstairs to their duties with the dancers. The singers, it seems, sang well, but could not make themselves heard before so crowded an audience on that long mill floor.

Other local mills and organisations contributed to the new Bailey Hall Mill inauguration : mosaics for the room where the tea was served came from Dean Clough Mills, crimson serge for decoration from Denison's Lee Bridge Mills, and flags and banners supplied by the Halifax Horticultural Society floated from the roof.

Nearby, in Navigation Road, the Flour Society erected a still more massive five-storey mill in 1879. The society is no more, but its two mills are still actively engaged in local industry.

When Blondin came to the Piece Hall.

MANY breathtaking tightrope acts have been performed in Halifax in the past, but never one that provided such a sensation as Blondin's that evening of August 23, 1861, when he demonstrated his prowess on the rope in a very unusual setting. Earlier that year he had astounded the world by walking a rope stretched over Niagara Falls, blindfold, carrying a man and enveloped in a sack. Nothing so limited in space as a big-top or a theatre would give Blondin scope for an exhibition, and his rope was stretched from opposite corners of the Piece Hall, sixty feet above the ground, being about 300 feet long—almost the length of North Bridge. Platforms had been erected on the walls at each end for the performer, who, high overhead, held the great audience spellbound, scared, amazed, fearful and relieved by turns as they gazed upwards.

Blondin treated his spectators to three exhibition feats. His first venture on to the long rope began as a slow walk, when, balancing a pole, he stepped along "with the ease and grace of a dancing-master." But after twenty yards slow advance he suddenly broke into a run, producing from the crowds a massed gasp, and as suddenly stopped and sat down on the rope. He lay on his back, somersaulted, swam, hung by his hands and legs, and stood on his head, beating time with his upraised legs to the music of the Black Dyke Mills Band. Regaining his feet, and the pole he had lashed to the rope, unneeded during these acts, he ran on to the opposite platform, to the admiring cheers of the assembly. His next feat was to walk the rope blindfolded, his body, as at Niagara, enveloped in a sack. During this act, Blondin repeatedly frightened the crowd by pretending to miss his footing. One leg would slip and be suspended below the rope as if it were impossible to recover it. His antics before he finally reached the platform left the audience laughing incredulously.

The final feat was more hazardous still, for Blondin appeared on the rope carrying a man strapped to his shoulders. There was no frisking about on this journey, and he traversed the hundred yards of swaying rope as quickly as the weight of his burden would allow. The crowd were uproarious in their applause, and there was a rush to see the great Blondin at close quarters when he descended. It was remarked that although he was obviously a strong man, he exhibited signs of the nerve strain he had undergone.

64

Schoolboys . . . and a dog in church.

YOU could not expect Sunday services in the old Ripponden Church to be wholly uneventful and solemn when schoolboys in their hundreds were regular attenders, from custom or compulsion, and they were not! At one period about ninety years ago from Mr. Dove's far-famed educational establishment at Making Place, Soyland, nearly 200 pupils were marched to the church each Sunday, accompanied by their 20 masters; from Barkisland Old Endowed School (founded nearly 300 years ago) went the scholars, the headmaster and his family, his assistant and the servants; and from Rishworth School also went nearly 100 pupils, masters and staff. And there were the National School scholars and the regular congregation.

Thus there was plenty to exercise the vigilance of the verger, who, we read, was very strict with the boys and was given to "nobbing" them with his wand when they misbehaved. To them revenge was sweet, and when three who felt they received excessive attention and punishment from him met him carrying water from the ancient well in Ripponden Bank the chance could not be missed : the verger was generously soused with the water he had collected.

A "drillmaster" from one of the schools had the duty of walking up and down the aisles during service to admonish the unruly and to collect inappropriate but very popular literature the boys liked to read during the peace of the sermons and other convenient periods of the service. Punishment was severe and the offenders' literature was forfeited; they had to be adept to conceal their illicit preoccupation from the eagle eye of the "drillmaster." One diverting occurrence must have brought joy to the heart of every schoolboy present. The cook at the Barkisland Endowed School was followed to the church one Sunday by the school dog, who no doubt regarded her as a useful friend. The collie would not be driven away when she arrived at the church, and, being ten minutes late owing to her efforts, in desperation she left him outside and entered, deciding no one else would follow so late.

But someone did follow shortly afterwards, and the dog slipped in. It ran about the church in search of her. In the old church was the high three-deck pulpit—the obvious place from which to get a view of the worshippers; and, eluding the sexton, the clerk and the parson, the intelligent animal ran up the steps to the top, where it reared up with its forefeet on the cushion and peered round. Seeing the cook, who was horrified, the collie bounded down, and (says the narrator of this true incident, a relative of the cook) " bounded from desk to desk into the pew and there stayed."

Halifax-bred dogs for Emperor Napoleon III.

DOGS have won many prizes and medals for their Halifax owners, but there can have been no more remarkable results from exhibiting dogs at a show than those that befell a local townsman in 1863. Mr. J. T. Riley was a breeder of retrievers, and he was producing dogs that became celebrated far and wide. The Paris International Dog Show was a high aim, but it was not too high for the ten retrievers and seven pups from Halifax Mr. Riley exhibited. Two of the former secured first and second prizes, against world-wide competition, and all his dogs except two he required to bring home were sold " at satisfactory prices."

But that was not all that happened to this Halifax exhibitor. On the second day there were 30,000 people at the show, and the many distinguished visitors were headed by the Emperor Napoleon III himself. When the Emperor sent for " the little Englishman, and conducted himself with the greatest affability," as was reported, Mr. Riley was, indeed, a proud man. The presentation of the medals given for prizes was conducted with great ceremonial, each competitor receiving a prize being announced by a fanfare of trumpets. The medal for the first prize was of finest solid gold, equal to eight sovereigns in weight, and the second was of solid silver.

Later in the week, Mr. Riley, who with his Yorkshire friends had been shown the sights of Paris under a special pass sent by courier from the Emperor, visited the Imperial kennels at the Palace at St. Cloud, and the model farms. Two of his dogs had been presented to the Emperor previously, and from their kennels they " gave a cordial welcome to their former owner." The party was conducted round the state apartments of the Palace, where every courtesy was shown them. Two valuable vases from the Sevres factory, which was also visited, were given to Mr. Riley by the Emperor.

There came also an invitation from Baron Rothschild, who had bought two of his retrievers, to visit his chateau at Ferrier with a friend and with the Paris representative of the " Illustrated London News." The castle was described by that journal as " the finest in Europe." Mr. Riley and his companions breakfasted with the baron, the meal consisting of twenty-five courses, and they watched the retrieving powers of the dogs being tried out on the estate with great success by the local keeper.

Before leaving Paris for home, Mr. Riley received an order from the Emperor for two pups from the next litter produced by " Bess " and " Royal," his two famous dogs he had declined to sell at the exhibition.

The Prince Consort Statue.

THE statue of Prince Albert and his charger can seldom have looked better within the memory of Halifax people than it appeared, all bright and burnished after its Coronation clean-up in 1953. It may have looked more imposing in its original setting, described at the time its erection was proposed as the most prominent position in the town. For some forty years the equestrian statue on its pedestal of Aberdeen granite stood in Ward's End, at its junction with Southgate, facing down Horton Street, and it was impressive to people coming into the town from the station—the way of entry of most at that time.

There were admirers everywhere of Queen Victoria's Consort, once her critical subjects came to realise his qualities and his loyalty; and this admiration was given wide expression after his death in 1861. Halifax was not backward in wishing to commemorate his name. At a public meeting convened by the Mayor, Mr. John Crossley, only two months after the Prince's death, it was resolved to have a bronze equestrian statue erected.

An artist-sculptor who had had engagements with Prince Albert, Mr. Thorneycroft, was selected to carry out the work, and he was said to have produced a most realistic likeness. Nimrod, the favourite horse often ridden by the Prince, was the model for his mount. The work cost about £1,400, the bronze statue being cast in Birmingham. Horse and rider, weighing one and a half tons, standing nine feet high on the eighteen-ton pedestal of similar height, were surrounded after erection by ornamental railings, four tall gas-lamps lighting the statue from the corners after dusk. The Prince is portrayed in the act of receiving public honours, bearing a scroll in his hand, and wearing the Order of the Garter over his frock-coat. The inauguration on September 17, 1864— the date having been decided at a meeting in the new Town Hall— was preceded by a procession through the town, accompanied by the band of the 2nd West Riding Yeomanry Cavalry. Flags and ever-greens were strewn about the monument and streamers decorated South-gate and adjacent streets. Sir Francis Crossley declared that Halifax was the foremost town in honouring the revered Prince by erecting a statue in his memory.

The time came when increasing traffic in the principal thorough-fares necessitated more room. Widening Ward's End was only a partial solution; and the coming of the electric trams in 1902 forced Prince Albert to be removed. The difficult task of transfer to the present Heath Road site attracted great local interest. For similar reasons the statue of Colonel Akroyd was removed from North Bridge to its appropriate position in the grounds of All Souls' Church.

Hazards of an auction sale.

BEFORE the demolition in 1861 of two of the overhanging timber-ribbed buildings in Crown Street—picturesque but no longer safe, and in the way of increasing traffic—an auction of the internal fixtures, timbers, piping, slates, etc., was held. The shops with house premises above were those labelled " Styring " and " Lawrence," pictures of which have been left to us with those of " Walton, saddler " and " Parker, druggist," the next two properties to come down.

In connection with the auction many people inspected the buildings, and a pleasant surprise awaited those who mounted to the flat roof of Mr. Styring's. There, above the gorge of the narrow street where vehicles almost ground against each other and pedestrians kept under the low overhanging storey for protection from them, was a roof garden, fresh and well set out. Here the occupiers had planned a private, peaceful retreat; Few, said the " Halifax Courier," knew of the existence of this novel garden. which was probably unique in the town. The auction was concerned with this, too. for its foundation was of lead—which sold for £32, quite a sum in 1861.

A very different surprise awaited the fifty people who, five weeks later, attended the auction of the stock-in-trade of a firm in Bath Parade, following their bankruptcy. The sale was conducted on the second floor of the firm's warehouse. While the tables and other furnishings were being offered. competition was side-tracked by greater competition under the feet of the buyers—an ominous creaking and crackling. The floor began to sink, and then it crashed down into the room below. A score of persons were pitched through the five yards opening. clinging vainly to each other for support, to the floor nine feet below, falling one upon another. The auctioneer went with them—as did the furniture collected about him!

People left on the solid portion of the floor escaped from the building, thinking it was collapsing. while the unfortunates below scrambled out, many " sick with fright and complaining of bruises and concussions." One gentleman, a principal of Bailey Hall Dyeworks, was " missing " for a short time, but a search by a broker among the debris of furniture revealed him buried under it, in great pain with a broken ankle and his other leg damaged. A former landlord of the Old Cock Hotel, whose arm was injured, also had to be attended by a surgeon who was called. It was discovered upon examination of the flooring that the joists were inserted only very slightly into the walls, and the weight of people and furniture had caused them to spring out of the cavities. The floor was pronounced " most unsafe," a verdict the victims did not dispute!

A real " White Christmas."

PRIME place in reports of Christmas in the past was, as to-day, given to the weather. Sometimes it was as seasonable and snowy as modern Christmas cards depict it. But often it was not, and the old-fashioned white Christmas that every age seems to credit to the past was frequently mourned. One of the real white kind occurred in Halifax in 1860. Outdoor activities were restricted by the snow that fell heavily and buried the town under a deep blanket; and movement was more difficult still during the great frost that preceded the snow. Halifax had been gripped in an icy temperature, the roads so slippery that " nobody ventured on them who need not." The Calder and the canal were frozen firmly, and people slid and skated on them for several days. There had been other compensations for those who ventured into town in the few days before Christmas. Food shops displayed tempting game and other Christmas fare in quantities " so profuse and super-abundant that it was good for the admiring eyes and the stomachs of those who gazed upon them."

On the night of Christmas Eve, undaunted by the severity of the snow and the frost, one or two bands set out to enliven the town and to " play Christmas in." Discordant notes produced by one musician instead of his usual " melodious strains," puzzled his fellow- bandsmen, and the discord became worse as the band plodded through the snow. Finally, the player discovered that the valves on his instrument had frozen hard down while he had been playing. A friendly cottage fire had to come to his aid before he could resume. The Parish Church bells chimed the Christmas hymn after the last stroke of twelve, and " all the town and country was so thick with snow," we read, " that the tune was better heard in every direction."

An unusual but very human incident occurred in the town on Boxing Day, four years later. Two neighbouring butchers " near the Market Place " were engaged in a private quarrel in one of their shops, and the inevitable knot of onlookers collected. (Shops were then open on Boxing Day). The crowd of witnesses annoyed the angry butchers, and one of them picked up a pail of water and threw it over them. It became the turn of the soaked Halifax shoppers to be angry, and one resourceful victim found a handy bucket of *hot* water. He sent this flying into the shop, bucket and contents aimed at the pair inside. Whether this returned Christmas compliment made the butchers forget their quarrel we are left to imagine; the crowd deemed discretion the better part of valour, it seems, for having hit they ran, and the breach of the peace remained unofficial.

Warley's "Wild Goose Chase."

WHEN strange objects, on occasion, flew over Halifax a century ago they produced fright in some of the inhabitants who had confidence only in machines that kept to the ground. We learn, for instance, of sudden alarm descending on peaceful Warley on September 24, 1860, when one of its inhabitants pointed out something flying in the sky that could not be identified. It was much too big to be a bird. It was "very like a whale," or some huge feathered monster. Others were more knowing, declaring the intruder was a wild goose which was lamed, because in its flight " it waddled so."

But alarm spread like wildfire, and a courier was sent to Sowerby Bridge for ammunition with which to " wing " the monster—which, whatever it was, must be destroyed! We are told that " a gallant army of wondering spectators pursued the mysterious harbinger of fate." There was a volley of musketry; but (fortunately) the target was well out of range. When in due time it was revealed as an air balloon sent aloft by railway contractors the alarm of the inhabitants, to whom it was an unknown sight, gradually subsided, and Warley's " wild goose chase " became nothing more than a nine days' wonder.

Twelve years earlier there had been a scene of even greater excitement a few miles down the Calder, when the river figured in another chase of an aerial intruder in which thousands of people took part. Some hundreds of them, the " Halifax Guardian " reported, waded across the river, regardless of getting wet, in their eagerness to reach the spot where the great balloon would descend and to see its intrepid aeronauts as they climbed out of the " basket."

Yet there were many among them who did not know it was a balloon; they had never seen one nor imagined such things existed. There were a father and his two sons, for instance. On the approach of the ungainly thing flying through the air the sons were ordered to " fetch t' gun!" And the trio started out in hot pursuit with their loaded double-barrelled gun. But they fell in with an acquaintance who had seen a balloon, and who told them, to their astonishment, that " t' little thing 'angin' daan 'ad a man or two in it." So they held their fire, though unbelieving, and watched the disappearing object with wondering eyes. They related how " if it 'adn't bin for Johnny they wod a' peppered it !"

The People's Park statues.

THE People's Park in Halifax will never again be the setting for an event such as occurred there just three years after its opening in 1857, though in recalling the occasion it may readily be believed that there could have been no summer display of bloom and colour beautifying the park comparable with the picture it presents a century later. Sir Francis Crossley's bountiful gift has been brought to its full perfection; the vista of colour and spaciousness and distant statuary viewed from Arden Road, for instance, is one that no one would expect to see in the heart of an industrial town.

On that August afternoon in 1860, twenty-five thousand people assembled for the ceremony of handing over the new statue of the donor " to the Mayor, Aldermen and Burgesses of the Borough of Halifax for proper keeping." Six days earlier, the statue had arrived in the town in the charge of its creator, Mr. Durham, the eminent London sculptor. It had been subscribed for by the public, about £1,100 having been raised; to contain it the massive recessed pavilion was provided by the town. Chiselled from pure Carrara marble, the statue of Sir Francis in his chair, holding the scroll representing his deed of gift of the park, was placed on its pedestal of blue Sicilian marble. The ten-foot monument, weighing four and a half tons, must have appeared very impressive when new, facing out on to the long statue-bordered terrace.

These other eight figure statues were the work of the Italian, Signor Francesco Bienaime, who was the sculptor of all the Crystal Palace statuary and of several statues at Chatsworth. They represent classical subjects, most being copies of sculpture in famous places, some of them rare, and they, too, are of Carrara marble. Through a century's exposure to Halifax weather they have added an unusual dignity to the 12-acre park which Sir Joseph Paxton, the designer of the Crystal Palace, had planned for Sir Francis Crossley. The two naval cannons which for so long stood on the terrace were captured from the Russians at the siege of Sebastopol in 1854.

The statue inauguration day was a public holiday for Halifax. Bands played in the park, where the central pond fountain and hundreds of flags helped to make the scene a gay one. The ceremony, at which the sculptor was on the platform in front of the pavilion, was preceded by a procession of specially chosen contingents. This was headed by the Black Dyke Mills Band, which had already achieved fame, for it had recently been pronounced at the Crystal Palace the premier band of England.

Famous Aquatic Performer at the Park Baths.

UNDER-WATER antics would hardly be one of the expected attractions of Halifax at any time; but the balloonists, the tightrope walkers, the circus acrobats and the down-to-earth entertainers with all the thrills they provided gave no more eccentric performance than was witnessed at Park Road Baths on September 16, 1859. The "Gentlemen's 1st Class Swimming Bath," just completed, had been formally opened, and the Mayor, the magistrates and members of the Town Council were included in the assembled company. For forty minutes they watched the best swimmer in the world, as Professor Poulton was pronounced, perform the most astounding aquatic feats.

Sixteen exhibition items he gave in the 60-foot bath—which as a preliminary proof of his prowess as a swimmer he covered in three strokes, the first two carrying him 40 feet. He swam the length of the bath feet first, turning a somersault en route. He swam it again with his hands and feet tied. He walked with his hands on the bath bottom, his feet protruding above water. Then there was spinning; somer-saulting 20 or 30 revolutions in quick succession; posturing in various representations; revolving his body in a circle with his feet forming the centre; displaying the Indian method of crossing a rapidly flowing river; with several ornamental items for good measure, not forgetting his stand-ing plunge of 40 feet on the surface. Then followed a display in which the aquatic professor ate a piece of sponge cake while immersed, after which he had handed to him a soda water bottle half filled with milk. On the surface he put the bottle opening in his mouth and settled down until only the inverted bottle was clear above water, the milk visibly disappearing as he drank. Apparently the meal had to be rounded off with a smoke, for he demanded his pipe—a long clay—which was filled and lighted. Then the happy professor, puffing serenely, submerged again until only his hand holding the pipe head was visible to the spectators. The smoke that rose with regularity was evidence that he was surviving this final grim exhibition, and he emerged to the resounding cheers of the watchers.

Whether the announcement after the display that the professor would attend the baths every Tuesday to teach swimming resulted in an influx of would-be learners we have not discovered. But no doubt there were aspirants in Halifax who would rise (or sink) to the bait of "eight or ten easy lessons, no matter what age, or how nervous of water" and pay the guinea charged by this sub-marine professor for his course, buoyed by the hope of surfacing after the tenth lesson. In response to popular demand, he gave a second performance three weeks later.

Dickens, Cobbett and Thackeray in Halifax.

CHARLES DICKENS was given an enthusiastic reception here when he gave a reading of his " Christmas Carol " to a large audience in the Odd Fellows' Hall on September 16, 1858. Throughout the two hours this occupied, we are told, the interest of the audience never flagged; the breathless silences prevailing during the pathetic portions were relieved by the laughter that greeted the flashes of wit and humour that " sparkled like jewels " as they came from the reader, and by the applause that broke out at each great truth with which the narrative abounds. For Dickens, the " Courier " reporter declared, had as a reader great power, with a quiet, unpretending manner and correct feeling, producing great effect without any theatrical mannerisms. He was then forty-six. "A Tale of Two Cities," " Great Expectations " and " Our Mutual Friend " were not yet written.

Dickens had visited America when he was thirty, and had offended many citizens of the States by what he wrote following his visit. No doubt some Halifax citizens were offended by his patronising comments after his appearance here—when, according to the " Dickensian," he wrote of this visit : " Halifax was too small for us. I never saw such an audience, though. They were really worth reading to for nothing, though I didn't do exactly that. It is as horrible a place as I ever saw, I think." (He had *not* exactly read for nothing : he collected £70 !) William Cobbett had kinder things to say after his lecture in the Halifax Theatre in 1830 when on his famous " rural ride." "A finer audience, more opulent in appearance, better pleased, and above all things more attentive, I have not met with," he wrote. And he had not, like Dickens, personal connection with Halifax. Mrs. Dickens was the daughter of Mr. George Hogarth, who twenty-six years earlier had been the first editor of the " Halifax Guardian."

Thackeray had lectured in Halifax the previous year, 1857. It is recorded in reminiscences gleaned from letters of this other great Victorian novelist, edited by his grand-daughter, Mrs. Ritchie, that from the White Swan Inn, where he stayed, he wrote in humorous vein to his daughters, saying he " was feeling better, having just eaten two wings of a fowl for dinner and wished the pore bird had four." Thackeray had been attended by a Halifax doctor, and he wrote of him : " I think the doctor I have had here is the best of them all. His name is Garlick, and I like him both in cookery and as a medical man." He also liked a set of mugs in his room at the inn, for he used them as models for a " Valentine " to send to his daughters.

73

Bear hunt in the Markets.

HALIFAX revelled in fairs, menageries and circuses in the 18th and 19th centuries, and during the fairs many streets and open spaces were thronged with booths and roundabouts and swings and stalls. From the field by the Northgate Hotel, a popular place for outdoor revelry, to Horton Street, and from Woolshops to Cow Green, according to the type of visiting entertainment, Halifax besported itself. The Piece Hall served for galas and special demonstrations for over 100 years until the eighteen-nineties, the open Markets (covered in for certain events) for visiting menageries until rather earlier in last century. These latter were fairground circuses, and a feature was the dancing bear that was taken round the streets to herald the show—an expected " turn " that was as popular as it was attractive as an advertisement.

In September, 1858, a performing bear was brought to dance outside the circus enclosure below the Markets as an enticement to the strolling crowds. But this bear created enough unrehearsed excitement outside. He refused to dance, instead suddenly bolting down the steps into the street. The startled crowd that was assembling scattered before the beast, who ran wildly about the street and then into the Markets. Its owner and some assistants, with those from the crowd who dared venture, dashed in after him. The hue and cry attracted more bear-hunters, who were reinforced by the nearby butchers armed with cleavers and other tools of their trade in readiness for all emergencies. The " Courier " account reveals that the bear had been " out of sorts " all day; having to dance for the people was the last straw, so he took steps, literally, to get out of it, and made the people dance about instead! The chase ended without serious casualty, the bear being captured by the menagerie officials and enticed back to his quarters.

Human freaks, dwarfs and giants, the heaviest and fattest men and women, were ever popular as side-exhibits. And if they could perform something wonderful as well they were famous. One such " star " who enthralled his Halifax audiences was the seven-foot-five Belzoni, who exhibited his great strength at a circus in the Markets more than 100 years ago. This giant's speciality was to appear with a wild beast's skin thrown over him and with an elaborate iron contraption fastened round his body. He would invite ten men to take up their stand on this appliance, and then Belzoni would march around carrying his ten-men burden—a human pyramid—in an impressive style that such a feat demanded.

Landslide at Stump Cross.

THAT Sunday night of December 6, 1856, was an alarming and an unenviable one for the few people then living at the foot of Shibden Valley where it merges into Stump Cross. After a heavy snowfall there had been a sudden thaw on the Friday, and much rain had fallen since. About midnight on the Sunday people were awakened by rumbling noises that brought most of them from their beds in panic. The upper part of the steep hillside began to slide towards the valley, gathering with it as it descended, trees and large stones and a tremendous weight of earth and sludge.

But this was not known at the time. Not until daylight could it be seen precisely what had happened during the night, nor the extent of the damage be discovered. It was then found that the wood on the upper part of the hillside had entirely disappeared, all the trees having been uprooted and carried down under the pressure of the slipping soil to the roadway at the bottom. Twenty yards of the road itself had been forced ten yards from its original position, but it had remained more or less intact. Fences and walls had been torn down, and the whole locality looked as if it had been the scene of an earthquake.

On the lower slope earth seemed to have been pushed upwards, reports stated, under the pressure from the slipping hillside; it was piled with trees, tree roots and blocks of stone. Streams of sludge were oozing down Brow Lane, and as this collected near the Stump Cross Inn a plank had to be laid to the back entrance.

There had been no serious injury to anyone, but several people had narrow escapes. Three young men, one of whom was the son of the toll-bar keeper at Stump Cross, were up on the hill when the landslide started. They sank up to their thighs in the wet soil and sludge as the ground gave way under them, and they had difficulty in extricating themselves from the slipping mass. A pedestrian on the road at the foot declared that he had had to " run for his life " to escape from the descending mass.

The previous year there had been a minor landslide near the hilltop, which had left a crevice ten feet deep, and the accumulation of water in this long, deep hole, seeping under the soil, and the pressure of earth higher up, were believed to be the source of this 1856 landslide.

Pair of oxen roasted in Piece Hall.

THAT was a great day in Halifax—the roasting of the two oxen as part of the celebration here of peace with Russia on May 29, 1856, but it was a novel and most important one, and 8,000 people tasted the meat. Nine field-pieces of artillery on Beacon Hill, with fireworks and a bonfire, were impressive enough, but the cooking of the oxen was as fascinating a spectacle as it would be to-day in the same setting. Each weighing 67 stones and costing £56, selected by local butchers, the beasts were paraded through the town headed by a band and attended by an immense crowd, to the slaughter-house. There they were killed by the most humane method known so as to be fitted for roasting whole, and were then hung for " viewing " by sightseers.

In the Piece Hall coke fires had been piled between iron gratings and brickwork. They were lighted in the afternoon in the inevitable heavy rain, which did not prevent the crowds of spectators awaiting the arrival-in-state of the first carcase. This appeared at 10 p.m., and was put up on the crossbar amid great shouts. The other was brought in at 1 a.m. The contraption allowed for rotating for even roasting : the pedestals had been cast by Mr. Berry in his New Bank foundry. Drip pans underneath caught the fat, assistants with long-handled ladles scooping the hot liquid and deluging the hissing carcases.

The firelight illuminated the whole Piece Hall and surrounding galleries with a ruddy glow, revealing thousands of spectators. More than twenty butchers were in attendance, basting the rotating roasts and hurrying about in the rain with their naptha lamps. A night force of police cleared the spectators, but roasting proceeded throughout the night : and until 6 p.m. the next day it continued, increasing crowds watching the cooks. Then the meat was declared to be " enough," and was taken down to be dressed for the procession.

At noon the following day, the artillery on Beacon Hill crashed out and the church bells pealed. Everybody who could be on Skircoat Moor was there—and saw the two oxen arrive in the procession, on separate lorries, each drawn by four gaily caparisoned horses in file. The carvers were with them, making great display with their knives to whet the appetites of the watchers.

Back to the Piece Hall went the procession after due ceremony and parading, and there, before a concert given by thirteen brass bands, the oxen were eaten, in the form of 8,000 sandwiches distributed to those who were the holders of threepenny tickets of admission.

The flood on North Bridge.

THERE can hardly have been a more extraordinary flood episode than that produced by a storm in Halifax on July 23, 1855. For two days the air had been oppressively hot, and when this culminated in a red lurid sky on the second afternoon a storm was expected, but nothing so tropical in violence as that which burst upon the town at 6 p.m. For four hours the deluge was unceasing, and for a time lightning and thunder concentrated over the town.

Halifax was in process of being provided with improved drainage, and many streets were in a state of excavation, with uncompleted drains. Water poured into cavities in such volume that roadways were undermined, and old pipes still intact had little effect on the flood water. Cellars and shops and dwellings in Woolshops, where rivers of water converged, were flooded, and in the extreme lower part of the town twelve feet of water was swirling in places. Two people were drowned, one man being found in the Calder three miles from where he was washed away by the swollen Hebble which flooded all the mills and buildings on its course. It had risen rapidly to a depth of seven feet.

On to the stone bridge crossing the Hebble—the predecessor of the present North Bridge, and rather lower in level—water rushed in immense volume from Haley Hill, Range Bank and New Bank, and could not get away. The bridge was impassable, except by carters, who braved the passage on their horses' backs; and as the water rose to the top of the stone balustrades hundreds of people trying to get into the town were stranded at the New Bank approach to the bridge. Before them was a lake, 100 yards long.

Then it happened. The parapet for a third of the length of the bridge collapsed under the pressure, and crashed to the ground 50 feet below. The pent-up water poured through the gap in a tremendous cataract—the main cause of the Hebble's phenomenal rise. Some of the stone fell through the roof of a dyehouse, some on to a beerhouse called All Nations, where barrels were left floating in the flooded cellars. A gas pipe crossing the "brook" lower down was burst away, cutting off the supply for the flooded lower part of the town, and darkness added to the hardships, and hampered rescue efforts.

It was 10 p.m. before the worst was over and the rain lessened. During the four hours the new Ogden Reservoir rose from 10 feet to 36 feet. Danger precautions were taken, and the embankment withstood its first terrific test.

" V.I.P's. " come to Town.

IN August, 1854, a flower, vegetable and agricultural show was held in the Piece Hall, Halifax.   Like its successor just a century later in Shibden Park, this 16th Annual Exhibition of the Calder Vale Agricultural Society was an event of the season.   During the morning, the Mayor's carriage, drawn by four handsome greys, went to the station to meet the Lord Mayor of London, who was travelling " by the express from Huddersfield " to come to the show.   Amid the general excitement he was driven to the Piece Hall, and with his civic escort looked round the exhibits.   The carriage drove him to the Mayor's residence for luncheon, and later to Bradford, where he was honouring a Mayoral banquet.

The Halifax story of the last century abounds in " V.I.P." visitations —visits by Royalty, ambassadors and others.   And there were Royal army commanders like the Duke of Connaught, who came in command of a detachment of the 7th Hussars in July, 1876.   With his fellow officers he dined at Bermerside, the residence of the Mayor.   In 1889, the Duke of Clarence came to present new Colours to the 3rd and 4th Militia Battalions of the Duke of Wellington's Regiment, at their camp on the racecourse at Highroad Well.   The Duke of Norfolk called to see the Piece Hall in June, 1892, and wrote in high praise of it.   Most of the great political figures of the times, and the explorers, actors and writers, came to Halifax—a long succession which included John Bright, Richard Cobden, Livingstone, Stanley, Moffat, Henry Irving, Wilson Barrett, Dickens, Thackeray, Wordsworth, to name a few over a narrow range of years.

In 1895 came King Khama of Bechuana with a suite of dusky chiefs and attendants, and at a meeting in the Mechanics' Hall, presided over by the Mayor, he pleaded his case against his country being administered by the Chartered Company of South Africa.

The famous Russian revolutionary writer, Prince Kropotkin, a refugee from the Tsarist regime, gave the second lecture for the Sunday Lecture Society in 1898, packing the same hall to capacity.   He stayed at The Gleddings.

Twenty-two-inch-tall " General " Tom Thumb held three " levees " a day here during a visit in November, 1857, giving his remarkable impersonations of Napoleon, Frederick the Great, and other international figures.   His wife was about the same height, and they travelled in a miniature carriage drawn by two small goats—the entire equippage being tucked easily in first-class compartments on their railway journeys.

First Yorkshire brass band contest.

HALIFAX Piece Hall was the setting for the first Yorkshire band contest, on August 26, 1854, and from far and near people assembled to hear the competing bands in the fine weather which favoured the event. The judges, the report of this contest says, were "three gentlemen in whose good judgment anyone who knows them will at once confide, and more so when told that they were in a position in which, though they could hear, they could not see the bands.

If they did not see the "eighteen fine-looking young men, being also young in the art," forming the Waterloo Band from Brighouse, who were favourites with the audience, this did not prevent the young musicians receiving high praise from them. But this band spoiled its chance for a prize by its indifferent rendering of the "Hallelujah Chorus," its second piece.

The leader of another band, we read, "should have had the good taste to modify his tone and make it equal in weight to the rest of the band." In spite of this censure, this band, Pratt's, also from Brighouse, won the third prize, so beautifully did it perform a glee which was one of the gems of the evening. The performances of other bands from Airedale and Heckmondwike were "minus due merit."

The Clayton Band carried off the second prize, and the Borough Band from Bury the fourth. Dewsbury Band was the last to perform; and, by its "evenness of time, sweetness of tone and perfect harmony," was judged to be undisputably the first prize winner. This event, commented the "Courier" afterwards, "provided for our good old town a treat of high character," which it was hoped would be repeated many times.

Two years later, in 1856, a season of open-air band performances was inaugurated on Skircoat Moor, on Sunday afternoons. Subscriptions had been solicited for several weeks previously, the total estimated expenses for the 14 weeks being about £35. The Mixenden and Queenshead Bands alternated in providing concerts for this first season. Rain "fell plentifully," when Mixenden opened on June 22, but an audience of 1,200 listened to this novel outside entertainment.

After the first concert, protests were raised against this "violation of the Sabbath," but they did not prevail. The following year the People's Park was opened—and Sunday afternoon band concerts have since become a regular feature.

A " last train " to Bradford.

IT was not an apparition that emerged after midnight from a railway
tunnel a few miles from Halifax one Sunday in 1853.   A former
Lancashire and Yorkshire railway superintendent, Mr. Thomas Normington, who spent his retirement here and who died in his nineties, related
what happened in his early days when he was in charge of the last train
to Bradford one Saturday night.   The journey was uneventful as far as
Low Moor, but there the engine broke down.   In 1853 there were no
telephones, and the nearest spare engine was in the sheds at Mirfield,
Normington knew.   It was midnight, and the stationmaster told him
that no engine would come into Low Moor before nine o'clock the next
morning.   There seemed no alternative for his passengers but a walk
of three miles along the track to Bradford, or four by road, no conveyance being available at that hour of night.   But our Mr. Normington
was a resourceful young man of 29 then, and he was determined to get
his charges to their destination.

In those early days horses were used for the shunting of trucks.
Normington had an idea, and he used his persuasion on the stationmaster.   A shunting horse was roused from its week-end rest, harnessed
to a selected railway carriage that had a good brake, and the passengers
were assembled in the single carriage.   With a man leading it along the
dark track, the horse drew the carriage out of Low Moor, through the
thousand yards long Bowling Tunnel, to the top of the gradient at
Bradford Bank Top.   Here the horse was released, and the carriage
travelled alone for two miles down the one-in-fifty gradient, arriving
safely in Bradford Station at 1-30 on the Sunday morning.   An un-
orthodox mode of travel even then, when this section of the line was
only three years old, but an improvement on the method of progress
over the section from Low Moor.

While he was stationmaster at Sowerby Bridge, Mr. Normington's
staff had on one occasion to assist " four truckloads of incapables " off
the platform from a convoy of excursion trains returning from Liverpool.
This was an annual celebration, so he had his staff prepared for this
invasion, with the trucks ready to ship the " incapables " off the station
premises.   Incidentally, he had the distinction of rising from porter to
divisional superintendent in 14 years; and on his retirement after almost
fifty years' service, a casket containing a gold watch and £610 in gold
raised by subscription was presented to him.

Round of the town a century ago.

THE final "field day" for 1853 of the Ancient Halifax Philanthropic Society of Archers was held on Skircoat Moor, and while this was not remarkable then as an annual event it would provide a novel sight to-day. We are told there was good shooting, in bad weather, and a fine supper afterwards at the Golden Lion to round off the day's archery. Cabs were available to take the archers home—these rather unwieldy four-wheelers had been in use in Halifax for five years. They were soon ousted in popularity by the "Hansom's Patent Cabs," introduced by the enterprising Mr. James Lynch, who one morning in 1858 had two of his new cabs driven in style about the town, bringing one to a stand for hire in Waterhouse Street and the other at Ward's End. These early hansoms were also four-wheelers, but they were reported to be "as neat and tidy a turnout as Mr. Lynch ever ordered or as Mr. Hope the coachbuilder ever built."

The Corporation's new fire brigade had a great day in 1853, when its fire engine, "Amazon," was tried out for the first time at King Cross. It was 20 feet long, weighed two tons, and 40 men were required to man it fully. It had 720 feet of woven and leather hose. The suction pipes could draw from a depth of 24 feet, and a ton of water a minute could be thrown in two jets a hundred feet high—sufficient to reach the roof of our highest building.

A "Pitch and Toss" party ascended Beacon Hill about that time to play their forbidden game free from interference. But a suspecting constable surprised them, and they were charged. Their claim that they were only "pitching stones at the beacon" did not prevent the magistrates fining them 3s. 4d. each.

Under a practice introduced 50 years earlier, fines for wrongdoing provided bread for the hungry and workless. Thus, when six people were found playing with a football one Sunday, their fines of 3s. 4d. together provided 40 sixpenny loaves for as many poor widows; in 1811 a fine inflicted under the Game Laws had allowed 55 shilling loaves to be distributed in Ovenden.

The Fish Market in Halifax was famed among neighbouring towns a century ago. Boundless supplies of fish were on sale, with a large surplus for "export" to adjacent places. A market report in the "Halifax Guardian," in July, 1863 (when the population was about one-third its present figure), stated that "during the past week no less than 5,000 pounds of salmon alone was sold."

Poste haste!

IF you slipped down to the Halifax General Post Office at 5 p.m. one day and asked for your letters which had been posted in London that morning, because you wished to reply before you closed your place of business for the night, you would run the risk of being regarded as something not of this world. But long before the Post Office was erected—more than a century ago, in fact—you could have done that without your request appearing in any way odd.

In 1852, business interests here complained that the 7 p.m. arrival of the London mail posted at 9-30 a.m. was much too late, and hindered competition with rival firms in places that were much better served.

They protested to such effect that improved postal services announced in the "Halifax Guardian" in May of that year included rail arrangements for letters from the 9-30 London dispatch to be in Halifax by 4-45 p.m. and to be available for callers at five o'clock. Although this was before Halifax was served by a main line railway it was not regarded as more than a deserved facility that enabled business mail to be dealt with as it should be!

Lest we find ourselves thinking that this was a miracle that could not happen to-day, in spite of a hundred years of development, we might recollect the insignificance of the quantity of mail then compared with the vast amount handled to-day.

As for the Post Office itself, it is interesting to recall that postal headquarters here have moved about almost as frequently as players in the old party game of "General Post." The new extensions behind the Post Office add another link to the chain of local postal expansion measures. The "General" was opened in 1887, and it provided ample space for expanding business; forty years later the premises had to be greatly enlarged to accommodate the automatic telephone exchange. Previously, the Post Office occupied premises in George Street next above those of the Union Bank in part of what is now Somerset House.

When the move to these offices was made in 1863, it was stated that they were much more commodious than the former premises, the next below the bank, and that all business could there be transacted at a counter and standing in a draughty passage be avoided. The earlier offices in George Street had been occupied only a few years following the Post Office removal there from 10 Cheapside.

Premises in Winding Road had been vacated in 1837, back in the mail coach days, and in 1823, No. 6 Westgate housed the Post Office—when a postmistress was in charge and one man was sufficient to deliver the Halifax mail.

A " miraculous cure " of a century ago.

ONE of the almost incredible medicinal " inventions " that the dawn of the Electrical Age produced was advertised as obtainable from two chemists in Halifax a hundred years ago. If you had suffered aches and pains in 1852 you could have called with advantage at Mr. Thompson's shop at 1 Bath Parade—so well-placed in its heyday near the open-air bathing pool and the gardens beside the Hebble. The riverside resort had recently vanished, it is true, but this would not have mattered, for at the shop you could have bought for 4s. 6d. a Pulvermacher's Patent Portable Hydro-Electric Chain for Personal Use. Or, if you were a customer of Mr. W. Dyer, whose shop at 1 Corn Market is discernible in several of those pictures of Old Halifax, he would have sold you one.

It would have been " a good buy," one would think from this distance in time, for it was announced to be " the most wonderful discovery in Medicine and Electricity of the present day." It was devised for wear under the garments, and would relieve without shock or disagreeable sensation " instantaneously the moment it is applied " acute nervous pains such as head, ear and toothache, and rheumatic pains of all kinds. However long gout, tic, liver disorders, local paralysis or nervous complaints had spoiled your life, by the " continuous and perceptible action on the body " of this appliance they would vanish as if by a miracle. The chain would do other things, too, of a non-personal nature, such as precipitating metals from their solutions, decomposing water, and deflecting the magnetic needle. These simple achievements were included in the sweeping claim that " in short, it shows all the phenomena of a powerful voltage pile."

The instrument producing these astounding effects weighed two ounces, could be folded in a pocket-book or reticule for immediate use, and it would last a man his lifetime, " guarding himself, his family and his friends against that immense number of complaints and diseases in which mild streaming electricity is a perfectly safe, certain and wonderfully speedy remedy." Further convincing assurances before you invested your 4s. 6d. in this life-cure were there for you; the invention had been exhibited with the greatest success before the Royal Colleges, the Royal British Association, and other " Institutions of the Highest Class;" the chain was in use in most of the London hospitals; and testimonials in writing from the foremost men in the profession were available.

Gateway to the cathedrals.

|F in the middle of last century you had had occasion to stroll at night out of West Vale by the Saddleworth Road you would have had to pass the quaint, low-roofed toll-bar. West Vale was then little more than a village, but it was beginning its rapid progression. This toll-bar was distinguished for its massive white gates, and the building bore the usual notice board, painted white with black lettering, setting out the tolls and fees for the various types of vehicles and cattle using the road. Not far beyond the gates, which were opened early in the morning and closed at nightfall, was a small dwelling from which a great noise announced the craft that was carried on there, and the name, " Joseph Fox, Tinsmith," was displayed on a small sign.

At that time householders had to fetch water from wells and milk from the farmers, so pails, cans and utensils of every kind were in great demand; when the mills came to West Vale the output from the very competent tinner increased. But at night the Fox hammer was silent, and the tools laid aside : you would have heard other sounds coming from the little building.

We are told in an old record by Mr. W. H. Stott, one who admired the activities of Joseph Fox, how, at night, " harmonious chords of sweet music floated from this place." Through the toll-gate music-loving friends from the village passed, went into the shop, and foregathering round the stove there they would sing for hours, with or without accompaniment on the harmonium the tinsmith had made for himself. Glees and solos, excerpts from " Messiah " and other works would be rehearsed, and from the sheer joy of giving expression to their common musical interest in the uninspiring setting of this tinner's shop, at least four from this group of friends passed to their musical careers in the superb settings of England's cathedrals.

We learn of one who went early into the choir of York Minster. passing soon to Durham Cathedral; he had a fifty-one years' record of cathedral singing. One sang in the cathedral at Chester for some years. Another who had this early musical " apprenticeship " at the tinner's was appointed to Ripon Cathdcral, and sang there until his retirement. A fourth secured the position of principal alto at Lincoln Cathedral. Said Mr. Stott—and Joseph Fox's descendants in the district to-day may proudly agree, as may other West Vale residents—" This quartet from our little village gave something to look back on with pride."

Mill steam boiler explosion.

IN the early days of steam boilers several serious explosions, some destructive to life and property, occurred in local mills. The worst disaster from this cause happened at the Lilly Lane Mill that stood by the Hebble, on a site now traversed by Waterside.

There were three boilers in the engine house, the four-storey mill being occupied by two firms in the name of Firth who shared the power provided by the single engine. On the afternoon of November 29th, 1850, the central boiler exploded when the mill was fully working. With one huge lift, we are told, the boiler raised the four floors above it, and the rooms were gutted with all they contained. Masses of spinning frames and other machines crashed down—with the thirty-five people working them, mostly women and children. Immediately all possible local effort at rescue was organised; infantry from the barracks moved down " to preserve order," but they proved more useful in extricating the trapped and in rendering aid to the injured. The Fire Brigade had a busy time with the burning material among the piled machinery. In this calamity ten people lost their lives and twenty-five were injured.

It was at 8-30 in the morning of November 16th, 1854, that Elland was shaken by the terrible explosion when the engine at Balmforth's mill was started up. The engine tenter had sounded the works' whistle, when without warning the boiler exploded with a tremendous report. The explosive force was so violent that the boiler was lifted from its bed through the engine-house to " an altitude as high again as the new mill." It was flung over the corner of the warehouse at the top of the mill yard and landed in a field 100 yards away, reports stated. An observer living near the field said the concussion was terrific, and the boiler flying over resembled a balloon. A large portion of the works was demolished, the boiler-house wrecked and a dye-house left in ruins.

The safety of the tall chimney was in question, expectation of its almost certain collapse adding to the risks of efforts at rescuing a group of victims trapped under the machinery. The chimney did crash a quarter of an hour after the explosion, smashing through the drying-house, and it was responsible for one of the four fatal casualties. Apart from these four killed there were only three reported injured; fortunately the calamity occurred immediately before the mill-hands, called by the whistle for the after-breakfast shift, entered the premises. The boiler involved in this Elland disaster was of thirty horse-power, that at the Lilly Lane Mill being of twenty-five.

The face on the chimney.

IN the early half of last century there was open unspoiled ground from St. James's Church as far as Stannary House; and at Stannary House, where card-making was carried on in the upper rooms, as was the practice of the day, there lived one who was proud of the pleasant outlook from his windows. The distant church was his friendly neighbour —until things happened . . . .

The card-maker was a man of spirit, it seems. And when the builders appeared and began to erect the first of the rows of houses on this space between his home and the church he gave vent to his feelings in no uncertain fashion. On the rising ground nearer the house the building proceeded, needless to say, without regard to his opinions : less and less of St. James's Church was visible as the houses at the top of what is now Crib Lane rose stone by stone, and his wrath increased proportionately.

Daily he visited the masons and rated them for what they were doing, but they went on earning their living and providing the houses. Their enterprising employer, according to a report of the time, said : "Never mind th' old chap! I'll plague him before we've done with him!" When the brand new houses were almost completed, our injured resident complained with final bitterness that he could now see nothing. This was where the builder took his revenge for all the months of complaining. "Oh, if tha' wants summat to look at tha' shall 'ave it." he retaliated. On the gable end of the fourth chimney at the top of Crib Lane he affixed a stone face—a carved, very ugly man's face, looking at Stannary House. Every time our defeated card-maker looked from his windows he would see this grinning adornment returning his gaze, and the chuckles of the builder over his questionable victory can be imagined.

The ugly face is there to-day, high up on the chimney side—too far distant from Stannary House, it might seem, to be a real annoyance, but it could be infuriating to the man who knew it was there as a permanent mocking affront to him. His eyes would be drawn to it. An incongruous ornament the face appears now weathered and indistinct on its old background. One wonders if ever eyes are drawn to it to-day : when newly-carved in light stone it must have prompted much questioning from passers-by who saw it for the first time.

Oratorio in the mill: First "Messiah" performance.

THERE can have been no music in a Halifax mill to compare with that arranged by the workpeople of the Akroyds of Bankfield on December 8, 1849. Up on the third floor of their great new mill at Bowling Dyke 2,000 people packed the entire floor for the great concert to celebrate the mill's completion. The combined orchestras and choirs under the leadership of Mr. Frobisher, a popular conductor who achieved more than local fame, rendered 27 selections from Haydn's "Creation." The Yorkshire "Queen of Song," Mrs. Sunderland, of whom the North was so proud a hundred years ago, thrilled everyone by her singing of "With Verdure Clad" and other arias. We are told that "the breathing of all the 2,000 persons seemed to be silenced at the extreme end of a room so long that the figures of the men and women crowded there seemed but those of little children."

Many other popular singers entertained, and Handel, Mozart and other composers were played and sung high up in that mill, making the murky air of Bowling Dyke resound with music. The room, it was said, was better adapted for such a musical concert than would have been believed. The "rare musical treat" provided for the people of Halifax in that unusual setting was for the benefit of the Infirmary.

Eighty-three years earlier Halifax had listened to "Messiah" for the first time. The Parish Church was the setting then, the occasion being the opening of the new organ in 1766, when on two successive days "with the Assistance of a Very Numerous Band of the Most Eminent Performers, both Vocal and Instrumental, from various parts of England, the Oratorio composed by Mr. Handel" was performed. This was just forty years after its composition. "Between the first and second acts" a concerto on the organ was played by William Herschel, who was appointed organist at the church following these performances. He left after a few months, however, to exercise his other interest that made him world famous, and fifty years later as the great astronomer he was knighted. George the Third visited and showed much personal interest in the ex-organist's great telescope at Slough that was one of the wonders of the early 19th century.

These "Messiah" renderings were held in the mornings. Tickets were sold at the White Lion, the White Swan and the Talbot Inns, and there were special assemblies at the last-named hostelry on the two evenings. The introducer and conductor of these first performances, Mr. Joah Bates, had the distinction eighteen years later of conducting the Handel Commemoration Concert in Westminster Abbey.

87

Victoria Reservoir.

AWAY from the town on the open highway known as Gibbet Lane, there was a newly constructed enterprise of real value and significance to Halifax people a century ago. For the people had built it—workers from the factories and mills, tradesmen and their apprentices, merchants' clerks—when the trades of the town were dying in the great depression. Unskilled labour it had been, largely, by the population who wanted work to keep themselves alive. In 1848 unemployment was causing destitution beyond the means of the Guardians to alleviate on the scale demanded. Meetings were held, processions organised, and the protests culminated in a demand by the workless for employment to be provided. It resulted finally in the trustees appointed by the Act of Parliament of 1823 deciding on the construction of a much-needed reservoir.

There were several springs supplying water to the town, but only a few tiny reservoirs, which would hardly be so generously named to-day. One was in the Old Cock Yard, another in Birks Hall Wood that stored only 500 gallons, and a larger one in Gibbet Hill on the site of the present Waterworks office. All these were already 80 or 90 years old. Two small reservoirs had been built in Hanson Lane following the 1823 Act, a third of the cost being met by private subscriptions, but water consumption by the population of about 23,000 was overtaking the supply in 1848.

So a new reservoir was the answer. A public subscription to help in paying the wages of the workers engaged—7s. per week—raised £1,500, about one-eighth of the total outlay including the cost of later alterations. More than 8,000 barrels of gunpowder were used to make the cavity and the foundations for the embankments. The reservoir was constructed to hold 14 million gallons, an outstanding capacity for the times, but later strengthening of the walls and improvements to the bed reduced its capacity by two million. With appropriate ceremony and seasonable rejoicing on Christmas Eve, 1849, the first water was run into the Victoria, named after the young Queen, and the " people's reservoir " was inaugurated.

Alas, not only was the labour unskilled; the engineer had little experience of such work, and before the reservoir would hold water, the bottom had to be reconstructed, hence the date on the stone.

In was the precursor of the enormous undertakings in the town's water storage. Ogden, nine years later, the first large reservoir, was nearly twenty times its size; several smaller ones followed, until the real giants began with Widdop, more than fifty times the Victoria's capacity, twenty years later again. " Victoria Reservoir, 1851," says the stone-lettered inscription on the well-known tessellated wall in Gibbet Street; and it is still serving the town a hundred years later—an example of the creation for the population, out of " temporary relief " of a project of lasting benefit.

The Railway comes to Halifax.

IF you had been curious enough on October 21, 1846, to follow a procession you found leaving the Northgate Hotel, you would have been in the company of " a greater number of wealthy and influential individuals than ever perambulated " Halifax streets in procession up to that time. The Beadle and the Constables who led the cavalcade finally halted it in a field near Canal Road, which was at the bottom of Horton Street, and, seeing the galaxy of beauty and fashion gathered on a platform there, you would have realised what a great occasion this was. The first sod for the line that would connect Halifax with Bradford and Leeds was about to be cut for the West Riding Union Railway.

After a speech by the Manchester and Leeds Railway chairman, you could have seen Her Majesty's Chancellor of the Exchequer presented with an inscribed spade. With this he " shaped out a sod very scientifically, with one thrust of his foot on the spade bringing it up and landing the sod safely in the barrow, amid loud cheers."

If you were not greatly impressed by this dexterity of the Chancellor, you had still to share the entertainment of the crowd in the next adventure of the turf. The barrow—a common one but quite new, we learn—" was seized by the Lord Viscount Morpeth, who trundled it at railway speed for a few yards," when he turned out the sod. This popular Minister of the Crown, too, drew cheers and laughter from the spectators by his efforts, and he delivered the empty barrow to the Chancellor, who mounted it for his speech. The happy scene was the beginning of serious business—the undertaking that tunnelled through Beacon Hill, spanned the valleys, built the embankments and carved the cuttings that provided the direct railway connection eastwards which Halifax needed for commercial survival.

When the North Dean (Greetland) line to Halifax was first laid only a single line of rails was put down. It was reported that the early engines were ill-adapted for the heavy traffic they had to haul; it was no uncommon thing for goods and passenger trains to run back down the incline right into Elland tunnel, where they had to be rescued and pushed back by locomotives from Elland.

Railway history was made three years only after the cutting of the sod by the Chancellor (the Rt. Hon. Charles Wood, who was for 31 years Member of Parliament for Halifax) by an invention perfected by a local man, Mr. Lewthwaite, which was far in advance of the times. This was a machine for printing railway tickets and giving consecutive numbers to them while it passed them through at a speed of 15,000 an hour. The new tickets were described as " exceedingly beautiful."

Luddite became beadle.

"WE shall never see his like again. He filled his clothes and his office well," they said of Jesse Ratcliffe, who achieved fame as the Halifax Beadle during the last twenty years of his adventurous life. For in the exercise of his duties he had become an institution. Of portly, even rotund, proportions, and dressed in the gorgeous uniform of light drab, scarlet and gold that his important office demanded a hundred years ago, he "seemed other than mortal," we are told. The exceeding gravity of his deportment when on duty, clad in his best apparel, was fine to see. It was the more remarkable because of the contrast it held with the jollity of his demeanour in his undress hours when engaged with his fellows with their foaming quarts between them!

Jesse was born in 1791, one of a number of children left with a mother whose husband had run away to be a soldier, like so many during the Napoleonic Wars, and he had very early to seek his own way of life. Nothing more unlikely could have been expected as his future career than the office of beadle, when as a young man apprenticed to a Huddersfield woollen cropper and finisher, he became embroiled with the Luddites. In the activities that prevailed against the introduction of machinery into the mills he was as determined as any to destroy the new frames and looms. He was one of the mob which stormed Cartwright's Rawfold Mill, near Cleckheaton, on the night of April 11, 1812. Hundreds of men, well armed with pistols, bludgeons and pikes, attacked the mill—and Jesse had his pistol, too. But he quickly dropped this into the canal (he was fond of relating in later years) when the attackers were put to flight by the handful of soldiers who were in the mill with Mr. Cartwright, and he escaped prosecution. A number of his confederates were hanged.

He returned to Halifax, and in due time he was acting as public prosecutor himself, in the West Riding Court—pocketing, it was reported, "numberless shillings for laying information against persons of whom he knew nothing near as much as the Man in the Moon." Upon a magistrate being appointed following the incorporation of Halifax he became crier of the court, and he was the mace-bearer to the first Mayor. But his appointment as beadle in 1846 had already brought him fame and had given full vent to his especial pomposity. Nobody who had seen Jesse Ratcliffe on great civic occasions could possibly forget him— and his ponderous "Oyez!", thrice repeated in his deep, strong voice, that preceded his proclamations. He was in his 77th year when he died on New Year's Day, 1867.

The great concert swindle.

THE new Odd Fellows Hall provided a fine setting for the popular concerts, lectures and entertainments that were offered to the people of Halifax in the middle of last century. There had been a grand " one night only " entertainment on an evening in April, 1845; and the following week people flocked to the hall for another, eager to see and hear the galaxy of talented artistes advertised. The handbills circulated in the town by the visiting promoter-manager had announced that his company comprised American vocalists, an actress from New York's Bowery Theatre, comedians, nigger dancers, a " Virginny polka," a negro phrenologist and a famous mimic and caricaturist. He had engaged the hall and had personally supervised the erection of a temporary platform to accommodate his large company. The charges for seats were to be only 2s., 1s. and 6d., and as so much was affered for so little there was no lack of patrons.

The concert was timed to begin at eight o'clock, but at eight-fifteen there was still no sign of the artistes. The audience became restive, so the promoter left the pay desk, where he had been taking their money, and announced that he would now bring on his company. But there *was* no company, and the producer had slipped from the hall after his announcement and had vanished—the proceeds of the promised show being certainly " takings " as far as he was concerned, for he took them with him !

The " Halifax Guardian " reporter suggested happily that this expert trickster performed in his own person the only song sung for that concert : " ' Off !' said the Stranger, ' Off, Off and Away !' ". The anger of the audience when they realised they had been cheated was difficult to restrain; but by the " vigorous exertion of several gentlemen " their revenge on the hall's fixtures and movables was prevented. After the hubbub had lasted some time the spirit of fun came uppermost, and the joker's trick was relished. It was appreciated the more when it was discovered that the songs in the promised programme bore such unlikely but appropriate titles as " The Absent Man," " I Calculate There'll be a Row," " Dinah, Dear, Him Go Away," and " Right Slick Away I Went."

This was declared at the time to be the cleverest and most audacious piece of swindling that had ever been tried on Yorkshiremen and had succeeded. The following day parties set off to Leeds to search for the trickster, but they did not find him. The real name, profession and place of residence of the perpetrator remained undiscovered.

Trouble at the Fair.

IT started on the Saturday night before the Summer Fair of June, 1845, really got going. Among the stalls and booths that had been erected below the Markets were several that exhibited articles to be won by " Wheels of Fortune," which besides operating notoriously against the victims who patronised them were against the law. To cope with the " rogues and vagabonds " who expected to find it profitable to operate these unlawful sideshows the two Constables the town proper then possessed called out the emergency arm of Special Constables, " captured " six of the law breakers and locked them up. Early on the Sunday, twenty or thirty other would-be offenders thought it prudent to rid the town of their presence, and did. At the Magistrates' Offices on the Monday, the six prisoners were committed to the House of Correction for a month.

On the Tuesday there was trouble at the Horse Fair, where the sales " sharpers " were in action; but in most cases it was not until later that the victims discovered they had been duped. One farmer sold a horse for £15, to find afterwards that he had been paid with spurious five-pound notes. Another bought for £19 a horse that proved to be worth only about £4. There were compensations, however, for the report of this fair, covering also the cattle and pig sales, states " we have not heard of a single pocket being picked."

The wide-scale trouble came on the Sunday after the closing of the Fair, which, said the " Halifax Guardian," " from time immemorial has been given over to pleasuring, drinking and vice." The streets had the appearance of a regular fair day, noisy with drum-beating and the " tom-foolery of pantomime," and the stalls were still displaying edibles. Trains and every kind of vehicle poured visitors into the town. Six thousand passengers travelled between Elland and Halifax on this Sunday, seven hundred more than on the Saturday. Some wild spirits brought disorder with them, others carried it elsewhere when they left. At Elland, for instance, two merry fellows in gigs used the old narrow bridge as a race-track for their vehicles on their return. They were both picked up unconscious when their gigs collided and overturned on the bridge.

There was a unique occasion when trouble-causers were collected—on a special afternoon during Revival meetings in June, 1864, three hundred men " of irregular habits, tipsters, gamblers, thieves, etc.," assembled in the Odd Fellows Hall. After being entertained to tea they were privately addressed by an evangelist.

The great temperance gala.

THE Halifax Summer Fair, normally thronged with crowds throughout its week's run, was so thinned in mid-week by the Temperance Gala's rival attractions in June, 1845, that it almost collapsed temporarily as a fair. Two men with a lively humour set out on the Thursday evening with lanterns to search for it! Neither the public-houses nor the pantomime booths were patronised as was their wont, we are told. But the events at the Temperance Gala were on such a grand scale, and so novel, that it was hardly likely that the familiar attractions of the fair could compete.

The gala opened on Wednesday, June 25, in the Piece Hall; and at four, five and six o'clock tea was provided for as many as wished to partake, at tables laid in the galleries. This was a popular and successful beginning. After it " three powerful bands of music stationed in the area commenced operations," the " Halifax Guardian " reported. Immediately the greensward which then covered the arena was crowded with dancers. Such a scene as followed in the Piece Hall had never before been witnessed. Quadrilles, waltzes and country dances progressed in the most approved fashion, we learn, and the polka was danced in ballroom style. During one set of quadrilles, 600 dancers " stepped the light fantastic toe " together, and the spectators were as delighted by the spectacle as were the dancers. There were other amusements— juvenile games and never-ending sources of fun and frolic that kept the merry-hearted affair going with untiring zeal, the bands playing throughout. It was to have been a one-day gala, but it was such a success that it was extended to Thursday and then to Friday. There was plenty to drink, but " no beverage was stronger than ginger-beer."

This gala was in keeping with the great part Bands of Hope and other temperance movements played in the life and events of the town. They organised reunions, anniversary gatherings and many other occasions, of which processions through the streets were popular features. The drunkenness that was rampant gave rise to the widespread efforts to combat it. At one meeting, the audience crowded into the Odd Fellows Hall to hear " the most brilliant temperance orator of all generations," an Englishman, but an American by adoption, famous in the States 100 years ago as an apostle of teetotalism. They listened to an address that, fully reported, would have filled eight closely printed " Guardian " columns. But then the speaker had the power " to make men weep like children, and women to sob as if their hearts would burst."

The Riding School.

"**A** RIDING SCHOOL that would exceed in its dimensions every other riding school in Yorkshire," was the aim for the building erected in 1844 in Halifax, " between St. John's Street and St. John's Lane." It was a substantial building 114 feet long, 64 feet wide, with an end gallery for 160 spectators. It had stabling at the rear for 15 horses. A carriageway, 16 feet wide (the forerunner of the present cul-de-sac behind the Electric Cinema), connected the two streets until St. John's Street disappeared under later development, and was the approach to the open space of 230 square yards in front of the entrance, allowing for proper assembly of riders and carriages. This carriage drive and forecourt were features that distinguished the riding school from every other public building in the town, it was declared with pride.

There was scope for instruction in horsemanship in a town of 22.000 people, numbers of whom stabled horses either at their homes or at the hostelries, and the Halifax Riding School promised this and more. It was completed on July 13. 1844. Besides its use for the tuition of horsemen and horsewomen, the long, enclosed arena became familiar to the mounts of the military based in this area. The Yeomanry Cavalry and other mounted regiments, with their riding masters, used the school for many years, and it was often referred to as the Cavalry Drill Hall.

But a period arrived when horses came no more to the Riding School—unless they came with the circuses that performed in the arena from time to time. The far sighted planners of 1844 had erected their building 30 feet high to allow for extension of the gallery all round, to accommodate a further 400 people; and for circuses the area floor could be adapted to seat 1,000 persons in addition. Vaudeville shows and various other entertainments extended the public usefulness of the old Riding School building. An exhibition of billiards was given by a former English champion on one occasion, and the " diorama," an exhibition of pictures on moving screens that had a popular vogue in the late 19th century, was introduced—a precursor of the development that was to follow. Some of these events and displays may be recalled by present Halifax people.

The building was empty and almost unused for some years until, on Saturday, July 30, 1910, it opened on its career as the Electric Theatre with the new "Animated Pictures," being the first theatre in Halifax to be opened solely as a cinema. Its first manager, Mr. Dearden, had been in charge of the American Skating Rink, opened three years previously near Clare Hall.

Omnibus horse won cavalry steeplechase.

"LIFE and spirit" were infused into Halifax by the Morley and Agbrigg Yeomanry Cavalry, it was stated in 1844; for too long society in the town had "lapsed into senility!" And when the regiment staged its steeplechase in that year in fields off the road to Leeds there was life and spirit in plenty. A handsome gold cup worth £80 was to be competed for, and there was a sweepstake of £5 each for the officers of the corps riding their own horses (no paid riders or grooms being allowed), with a handicap of two sovereigns each for non-commissioned officers and privates owning their own horses, to which the officers added £10.

The race was to start at one o'clock, but from early morning all roads leading to the ground selected, covering several miles of fields— some ploughed, some under stubble—were busy with pedestrians; by eleven o'clock they were a-block with vehicles from donkey carts to carriages. The course contained about forty leaps, some fences being declared fairly easy, but some hedges "regular raspers" and a few ditches real "yawners." A wide, deep pool was another obstacle. There was a grandstand for the elect, with a nearby field for their equippages, but the whole course was visible from the main road and it was stated that 30,000 people watched the exciting contest.

The regimental band, in full uniform, enlivened the long delay in starting. At eleven o'clock stewards had set out to inspect the course, and it took them two hours. They decided the course was much too long, had condemned several of the fences and walls as too dangerous, and it was four o'clock before the race could start—on a replanned course reduced to three miles, with 32 jumps. After the last leap a fine long run gave the horses a trial of speed to the winning-post. All but one, which lost its rider at the second fence and "found himself twelve-stone lighter" kept up with the rest far into the course, completed the race. There had been both scrambles and flying leaps across the pool.

Of the eleven horses competing, five, including the winner and the second, were owned by privates of the corps. The winner had three years previously been pronounced "done-up," and had been exchanged for a £10 note. For two years before the steeplechase he had pulled an omnibus. Once a good hunter, he had sprained a leg and was rendered unfit to be ridden. Omnibus-pulling had cured his ills and given him a new lease of life as a cavalry charger.

95

Well Head "Spa"

"THERE is no telling what the tastes of the people will lead them to," said our local paper in September, 1842. A large proportion of the population had of late gone "drinking-water mad," it appears, and the springs in the neighbourhood were visited early in the morning by thirsty and panting devotees who took their pints or more as a daily tonic. But one spring bubbling away in Well Head field in Halifax carried off the palm for popularity. (There is still a trough in this field supplied with ever-running water from the spring).

At the time of the "Guardian's" cheerful comment, the lane leading past Well Head from Harrison Lane, the outlet from the town at Barum Top, was crowded with water drinkers, we learn, who, with cans, pots, tankards and questionable drinking utensils, were to be seen hustling each other in their eagerness to reach the "Spa." And the satisfaction with which they had partaken of the sparkling waters was patent to all who saw their faces as they hastened back home for breakfast.

This new water-drinking craze, we read, was "the best mania with which certain of the population had been bewitched." Had they not at times previously taken to swallowing pills by the bushel, to rubbing themselves with brandy and salt, to taking physic until, tiring of it, they had thrown the surplus to the dogs? So now, more sensibly, they were quaffing from this pure stream. They should, said the helpful critic, ramble for an hour on Skircoat Moor either before or after taking the water (or without taking it, for that matter) to reap full benefit from inhaling the invigorating breezes. But at least a suitable entrance should be erected at the "Spa" for its protection!

As for the several "miraculous" cures already reported, the most wonderful repaired the ruined digestion of an aged woman from the low part of the town whose custom for years had been to lie abed until nine, smoke her pipe until noon, without having, for lack of appetite, partaken of breakfast. Persuaded to try the cure at "Well Head Spa," daily, she rose two hours earlier, threw her pipe aside, drank two glasses of the water, walked round "the Moor," drank again on her way home, and there ate a hearty breakfast.

The beneficial results for those who frequented this spring and its airy surroundings were not surprising; and if the water was given the credit, this, too, is understandable. It was a luxury, for in 1842 Halifax had only three very small storage reservoirs and two water tanks to serve its twenty-one thousand population.

The " Plug Plot " battles.

THE presence in Halifax on a fateful week-end in August, 1842, of troops from the 11th Hussars, the 17th Lancers and the 61st Regiment of Foot was considered insufficient protection for the town against the trouble that threatened from the approaching discontented operatives from Lancashire and from Bradford. So the magistrates swore in special constables, men even being called from places of worship on Sunday, August 14, to be appointed. The "trouble" was the widespread movement to stop the mills, in the agitation for the long-discussed Charter laying down satisfactory working conditions, guaranteed wage standards, etc., and as the method used by the "turn-outs" was to drive in the plugs of the recently installed boilers, the movement became known as the "Plug Plot."

The precautions were put to stern test. At 5 a.m. on the Monday a meeting of local operatives was held. It was interrupted by the magistrates and special constables, and broke up. But a procession formed from it to meet the 20,000 "turn-outs" making for the West Riding mills from Lancashire, who were known to be near. About the same time 5,000 from Bradford reached the town. They were met in New Bank by the magistrates, this time with the military. As they refused to disperse the Riot Act was read, with the desired effect—temporarily.

There followed meetings, clashes, clearing of streets by troops and a second reading of the Riot Act. Shops closed, and alarm spread in the town when the military fired on the mobs trying to prevent removal of apprehended rioters to the police office in Upper Kirkgate. In the evening 15,000 attended a meeting on Skircoat Moor, most of them camping there overnight, and at 6 a.m. on the Tuesday after another monster meeting, contingents set out to stop the mills. The biggest affray was occasioned by a contingent returning from Elland after stopping the mills there. Showers of stones greeted the soldiers and the police who met them, at the bottom of Salterhebble Hill. Many were injured, and three hussars were unseated, their horses running off. The troops then fired at the mob, some of whom were on the house roofs. At the top of the hill the infantry and the police were in action also, and there the magistrates declared their determination to clear the streets " be the consequence what it may." There were skirmishes near the mills in Haley Hill, sabre and shot wounds being inflicted, and also in the town, after further stoning of the military while rioters were being conducted to the lock-up.

The mills restarted on the Thursday, in response to a notice issued by the magistrates when quietness had been restored. Many rioters were sent to York Assizes, one from the Salterhebble battle being transported for ten years for assaulting and robbing a hussar.

The First Excursion from Sowerby Bridge.

THERE was no engine for an experimental journey over the new local
section of the Manchester and Leeds Railway in August, 1840, but
that did not hold up the excursion. Horses provided ample power—
and what an event it was! The population of Sowerby Bridge was
attracted by the novel spectacle. On the new bridge near the station,
the starting point of the trip, the train "of eight or nine wagons
beautifully fitted up and gaily decorated," was drawn up in readiness.
Special wagons were provided for "two powerful bands of music" to
enliven the excursion.

At eleven o'clock, the horses, with decorated trappings and gaily
dressed riders, were attached to the train. At a signal the bands struck
up "God Save the Queen," and to the cheers of the spectators the train
set out towards Mytholmroyd. We learn that at Luddenden Foot the
village band—"a regular old-fashioned set of musicians not particular to
the tuning of their clarinets"—played "See the Conquering Hero
Comes," as the gay train rolled slowly past. On to Mytholmroyd the
horses pulled the crowded train, the favoured travellers (standing in the
open wagons) receiving the plaudits of the line-side watchers—and the
ribald shouts of disapproving sceptics of the crazy new mode of travel,
of which it appears our countryside held many.

The return journey took the line towards Elland, progress down
the valley being "fine in the extreme" and the views from the train
enchanting. Crowds of watchers were seen to be lining The Rocks and
other points of eminence. On the bridge at Copley to greet the passing
train a fireman, a bugler, a clarinet player and a man with "a cracked
side drum" made themselves heard above the noise of the wheels. After
crossing the Calder and the canal, the passengers were plunged into the
darkness of the tunnel, but the train emerged safely into daylight to the
welcoming sound of the pealing Elland bells. Forward down the valley
to Brighouse, where similar excitement greeted the excursionists, whose
bands were playing in their best form, and round to Bradley Wood,
where the outward journey ended. Here "sumptuous entertainment
was provided by the spirited and noble-minded contractors"—a reward
appreciated by the intrepid travellers after their ordeal.

As for the return to Sowerby Bridge in the evening, several passengers
who were sceptical about night travel on the rails preferred to walk back
or to find some safer mode of transport. But their companions who
stuck to the railway arrived home with an unblemished record. The
only casualty occurred to a man who elected to travel home by omnibus:
he fell out, and was seriously injured.

The great Coronation feast.

THERE were a few Union Jacks as symbols of loyalty to the young
Victoria, but little other decoration on that June Coronation Day
in 1838. For Halifax had different ideas then for celebrating a coronation from those favoured in 1953. The bellman's cry in the town at
eleven o'clock the night before enjoined all shops to close throughout
the morrow, which was to be observed "by masters and men" as a
general holiday. The loyalty of the shopkeepers, we learn, "overcame
their worldly mindedness" and the town gave itself up to bustle and
excitement without the visible encouragement of bunting and illumination. For there was The Procession—a greater procession, surely, than
Halifax had ever seen or is likely to witness—and there was The Feast
that was to follow, when 3,000 people were to sit down to a roast beef
and plum pudding dinner in the open air of the Piece Hall!

The procession was two miles long, and with 6,000 people walking
or riding in it—for there were 425 horses as mounts or drawing the many
vehicles—it was an imposing demonstration. It took a full hour to pass
a given point. Early in its ranks were 306 horses, four abreast, on which
rode gentlemen of the town; there were the private carriages, and coaches
with four horses and postillions in red and blue jackets, and the assurance
companies' fire engines drawn by four horses, with their own postillions.
Bands, banners borne by members of various Orders, many of whom were
mounted; decorated wagons, a performing equestrian company in Grecian
costumes mounted upon their twenty horses. The band of this company
rode in their coach in the Sowerby Bridge section of the procession.

Breakfast had been provided for 3,000 Sunday school children before
they assembled for the march, each then proudly wearing their Coronation Medal; and the great event of the day awaited 3,000 adults when
the procession was over. This feast must have presented an impressive
spectacle. Sixty-six long tables were set out in the Piece Hall, where
"the most active gentry in the town and neighbourhood were employed,
one at the head and one at the foot, of each table, carving" and attending to the wants of the hungry diners. The prodigious quantities of
food and "the waiters, male and female," had been supplied by some
thirty of the inns and public-houses in the town.

And this Halifax multitude, who as a massed assembly with bands
had sung the National Anthem on Skircoat Moor before the procession
had moved off, did full justice to the honour of the young Queen Victoria
before they dispersed on that memorable 28th of June, 1838.

General Election riots.

GENERAL ELECTIONS came with a great onslaught in times past
and Halifax has experienced riots and battles between supporters
of opposing parties. Probably the most exciting were those that occurred
at the keenly contested election of 1835—there were scenes of wild
rioting difficult to imagine to-day. Even the day of nomination of the
three candidates for the two seats in Parliament Halifax was then allowed
was marked by scuffles and scenes that were described as a disgrace to
the town.

Long before ten o'clock on that New Year's Day morning, the hour
of nomination, the streets were lively with excited crowds, almost every
man and woman wearing colours. If one sporting a Tory blue favour
came up against one wearing a Whig yellow it needed less than a word
to start a scuffle. Bands marched up and down bedecked with blue
and yellow banners, the crowds accompanying them cheering and booing
according to the " party " of the committee rooms they were selecting
for their attentions.

The hustings were ready in the Piece Hall and thither the crowds
surged to hear the nominations and to join the excitement. When the
candidates entered, dramatically preceded by their bands—Sir John
Stuart Wortley, the Conservative " Blue," Messrs. Charles Wood and
Edward Protheroe, the Whig " Yellows "—there were 6,000 people in
the Piece Hall. Salutes of music, hisses and cheers greeted them. The
reading of the Writ, the Bribery Act and the administering of the oath
of office could not be heard because of the commotion.

But these scenes were mild compared with the wanton rioting that
occurred during the two polling days that followed. We read of " desperate outrages " being committed as rumours of voting reached various
parts of the town. The end of the second day brought reports that
Mr. Wood (later the Rt. Hon. Charles Wood, who represented Halifax
in Parliament for 31 years) had 336 votes, Sir John Wortley 308, and
Mr. Protheroe 307. That close result asked for trouble, and it came.

Most of the " outrages " were committed then—by a mob of 500
ruffians, reports stated, and wide destruction to property was caused.
The voting was officially confirmed in the Piece Hall the next morning,
and by that time hundreds of windows had been shattered at the principal
houses in the town, including the vicarage, regardless of the political
colours of the owners, but those of the Wortley supporters being especially singled out. Gigs and carriages were smashed, railings torn down,
and " breaking-in " gangs forced servants to take refuge in cellars while
they performed their misdeeds.

Claims for damage were many, and a special court at York Castle
sat for five hours assessing the awards of upwards of £2,000 for damages.

The open hustings in the Piece Hall were last used in the General
Election of 1868.

The Piece Hall " Sings "

THIRTEEN times the great Jubilee " Sings " filled the Halifax Piece Hall with people and the neighbourhood with the resounding song of thousands. From the first in 1831, to the last in 1890, at five-year intervals, they drew enormous gatherings of Sunday school scholars and teachers, choirs and bands. To have heard the singing of the hymns, led by the massed bands, on such a scale and in that setting was an experience almost beyond imagination to-day; but pictures may be glimpsed from records of some who attended—and who bemoaned their abandonment because of the new uses to which the Piece Hall was put for economic reasons.

The first jubilee mustered 10,000, and was so successful that the event became a feature of the town's life for sixty years. On that first occasion a gill of beer was awarded the singers with their buns, but this example does not appear to have been followed at later " Sings." An exception to the five-year interval was the repeat jubilee in 1863 in honour of the Prince of Wales when he came to open the new Town Hall. Then 20,000 children and teachers marched to their places in the Piece Hall, with the bandsmen and the choirs. Mr. Abel Dean, white-haired, with tasselled black velvet cap, conducted, using his yard-long thick white baton that all could see.

One thrilled spectator tells of the impressive scene when, the performers all assembled, " there came the entry of the cavalcade at the South Gate, the carriage drawn by prancing horses ridden by postillions, to the massed singing of ' God Bless the Prince of Wales '," and of the heavy downpour of rain which turned the whole assembly into a sea of open umbrellas !

Another great jubilee was in 1880, when the centenary of Sunday schools was celebrated by a still larger assembly, and when the Piece Hall was bedecked with flags and bunting. Such noble, sonorous singing of hymns could never be excelled, it was declared.

At the final jubilee 30,000 were in the area, including 600 vocalists to lead the scholars, and 500 instrumentalists, and the galleries held more than 8,000. Mr. Thomas Wadsworth, who harmonised many of the hymn tunes and arranged the band parts, conducted this jubilee.

Great excitement centred on the Piece Hall when Halifax gave itself up to the jubilees, whose fame attracted visitors from afar. Lively minor incidents, such as the chasing round the Piece Hall roof of two mischief-making youths on all fours by the police, as happened at one jubilee, added to the gaiety of the events. And at the end there was the refreshment of the vast throngs to be organised—itself an undertaking that, like the singing, is impossible to imagine now.

Panic in the chapel.

THE morning service began normally enough, but it broke up in pandemonium. The preacher was announcing the text for his sermon : "And the Lord opened the mouth of the ass, and she said unto Balaam . . ." when the congregation saw sudden terror in his face. They saw him flee down the steps and out through the side door. From his point of vantage he had seen the intruder entering the chapel by the front. On that fine Sunday in August, 1830, people had assembled at the Luddenden Dean Wesleyan Chapel from the sparsely populated hamlet and the farms on the hillsides as usual, many of them riding their jackasses, as their mounts were described by an eye-witness who graphically recorded what happened.

When the clattering of hooves shook the worshippers' attention from the text and the vanishing preacher, and an ass dashed into the chapel and kicked and pranced in the aisle, hooves crashing against the pews, there was panic. And can it be wondered at? Bees were swarming on and around the animal. There was frantic scrambling over pew tops by the alarmed congregation, whose single thought was to escape from the bees and the frightened animal.

Valiant efforts were made to quieten it by driving off the bees, which then tormented those worshippers who were not quick enough in escaping. But in time the truant swarm was collected and restored to the security of the hive. The poor animal, stung from head to rear, was led out to be nursed and pacified.

Bees ! As if a demented ass in chapel were not trial enough ! The reason was there outside for all to see. It seems that many of the people were beekeepers, for in those times beekeeping was common to most local farms. That Sunday fell in the season for the removal of the hives to the heather, and the chapel was near the favoured spots. So the owners combined business with worship and brought their hives with them, leading the animals which carried their precious burdens. In the " hive-piches " provided they placed their hives, and they left the animals to graze peacefully while they went to the service.

The ass that had caused the trouble had been innocently venturesome, it was plain to see, and had investigated the nearest hive. Resenting his intrusion, the bees had retaliated; and in his fury at being stung he had let out with his hooves and had overturned the hive—with the result we have heard. " What better refuge," asks our reporting eye-witness, " than the inviting open doors of the House of God, for poor Neddy in his extremity?"

Sowerby's 'whisht' and 'husht' shops.

THAT well-known landlord of the Star Inn at Sowerby styled himself in 1829 "Detector of Systematic Robbers," and "Thief catcher" was the way many people preferred to describe him; but "John Almighty" remained the most popular local nickname for John Whiteley. The other titles he earned by a complaint he aired in the "Halifax Chronicle" about the dangerous extent of the illegal sale of malt and spirituous liquors in Sowerby and Soyland.

Thirty-five houses there were in those townships alone, he said, which dissolute persons and even paupers in receipt of parish relief frequented. So concerned were many of the inhabitants by this illegal traffic that a subscription fund was raised for the prosecution of the law-breakers and a reward of five pounds was offered to informers leading to their conviction. Very soon two of the offenders were convicted and fined by the Halifax magistrates £14 10s. each for selling ale without a licence, and the informer received ten pounds.

"Nocturnal assemblies of paupers and other cheaters of the inn-keepers and the King," said the Star landlord, were held in these "whisht" houses or shops. Customers formed themselves into a secret society and could buy the forbidden "whisht" at any such house by giving a certain sign and password. They took a secret oath that they would not inform against the vendors for "husht" selling.

At these houses they would cook stolen game, hares, poultry and vegetables, and thieves and receivers of stolen produce met there, we are told, and "feasted in the night." On Sundays one customer watched in his turn at the locked door. In September, 1829, at a town meeting in Sowerby, it was agreed to enrol twenty-five special constables. A gang of drinkers returning from a "whisht" house broke into a grocer's shop, stole all his money and most of his stock. The Excise office at Halifax got into action, and during succeeding months many "husht" sellers were convicted and fined at the Halifax court.

But "John Almighty" himself was refused a renewal of his licence by the Halifax magistrates four years later. He appealed against this decision at the Quarter Sessions at Leeds in October, 1833, and got his licence renewed. He had frequently preached in a room adjoining his premises, and earlier that year he had delivered a lecture previously announced, on theology. There had been many people drinking in the inn at the same time, and it had been decided in the Halifax court that the lecture was a device to procure custom.

The Leeds magistrates were satisfied, however, by John Whiteley, who said he would never preach there again nor allow anyone else to.

So they broke the club rules!

THERE were rollicking sessions at some of the clubs formed in Halifax in the early 19th century, when people began to " club together " socially. Some of the earliest clubs were simply gatherings of the " rakes and blades " of the town; others at least set out with serious intentions —political, sporting, musical or purely social. They met at the popular inns, changing these frequently according to the extent of mine host's hospitality or his political colours.

The Ferry Bridge Court, formed for social aims about 1830, met at the Black Swan in Silver Street. A custom here that might not be popular in a modern club was to turn a member upside-down if he broke a rule; any coins that came to ground from his pockets were spent on drinks for the company present. Some club rules were so strict as regards gentility of behaviour that they were impossible, and things were made much livelier all round by the breaking of rules by members.

The Smoke Club, the Wool Club, the Colonial Club, all with their own peculiar rules, filled an active part in Halifax social life 100 years ago, as did another assembly of professional men and those of artistic and poetic leanings which included Branwell Brontë, of Haworth. The Chess Club was formed in 1840, and became famous with its contests with clubs of other towns. It took things very seriously, and under its rules no wines or spirits could be introduced and smoking was forbidden. At the Old Turk's Smoking Club a fine of sixpence was imposed for non-attendance, with a similar fine for failure to spend there at least sixpence per week on liquor and a penny on tobacco! Expulsion was the penalty if the fines were not paid. If a member became too quarrelsome he had to leave for the rest of the evening or pay a shilling fine. The fine money was to be expended at the annual dinner by the chairman for the comfort and conviviality of the members; from which it would seem that if members had kept the rules the feast would be a much less joyous occasion.

Special events had, of course, to be celebrated by a dinner. The young Queen Victoria, in 1841, provided an excuse for a convivial evening for the Old Turk's Smoking Club members, who, previous to the birth of the Queen's second child, registered a resolution. A dinner at the Turk's Head, in Old Market, was to be provided on the day following the birth " if the babe should be a Prince," the feast to include a couple of roasted geese, a leg of mutton and a tongue. The club got its dinner, and libations of liquor. The future King Edward VII had been born.!

The Godley Cutting.

IT is not easy to imagine Halifax without the familiar outlet via Godley Lane and Stump Cross, but so it was until the early 19th century. There was Shibden Hall Road ("Lister's Road") leading from Old Bank top and sweeping round past the front of the Hall and down into the valley, whence it rose towards Hipperholme; there was the ancient track over the shoulder of Beacon Hill, known long ago at the Halifax end as Whiskcombe Dandy, which was the beginning of the route to Wakefield. There was the steep rise over Range Bank which led ultimately towards Bradford; and, last but most used, the long climb up Haley Hill to Boothtown and beyond, the main turnpike to Bradford, with its toll-bar at North Bridge.

It was to save the coaches and other traffic the toil and dangers of this elevated route, which in winter was a source of many accidents and of snow-bound coaches, that an easier and shorter route was constructed leading directly from the town into the Shibden Valley. Thence the gradual rise to Northowram and the route along the valley to join the road to Leeds provided new arteries from Lancashire to the East, and brought greatly increased traffic through Halifax.

In 1827 the work of cutting through 800 yards of the rocky hillside began, and the filling up of the valley to complete the new roadway was not finished until 1830. The undertaking was declared one of the most stupendous of its kind in England. It involved lowering the high upper portion of New Bank and constructing Godley Road at an easier gradient (now crossed at the top by Godley Bridge). The cutting had then to be continued through solid rock for several hundred yards towards the valley. The total length of the undertaking was about threequarters of a mile. A line of rails carried trucks which conveyed excavated earth from the cutting to the raised section, and a score of horse-drawn wagons were continuously engaged. At its deepest point, the 44-feet wide cutting was 60 feet below the original level, and the road embankment at the highest point was 64 feet above the valley. The Stump Cross Inn's predecessor of the same name stood on a site now covered by the embankment.

Where the old Shibden Hall Road connects now with the main road below Hipperholme may be seen a stone in the wall bearing the date 1642, and inscribed : " Mr. Nathaniel Waterhouse Gave I.L.P.A. for the Repair of this Highway which the Intrusted Feoffees for Ever Must Pay." One pound per annum had some meaning 300 years ago, for the donor of this bequest was a most generous benefactor.

The Skircoat Moor stag hunt.

HALIFAX could always provide diversion, but none so unexpected as that provided one morning in 1824. Out of the greenery of Harrison Lane a hare suddenly appeared at Barum Top, and startled witnesses set off in full cry, joined in the chase by several dogs. Across into Cow Green the hare escaped, his pursuers close behind. Eluding his shouting and barking enemies, he darted into some open premises. Here the hunt became too hot, so he bolted out again and escaped down Copper Street. This street has disappeared since, as did the hare then, for the country was invitingly near. The hunters were outdistanced and saw him no more.

The stag-hunt was a more swagger affair, staged on Skircoat Moor in 1827 with much ceremony. A stag that had strayed, it was believed from Templenewsam, had been caught by some peasants and sold to " some gentlemen of Halifax," who handed him into the custody of a Mr. Moore, of Northowram Hall. For the hunt the stag was turned out on The Moor, before a company of nearly 300 horsemen, a pack of dogs, and " 3,000 foot people and numerous gentlemen's carriages filled with ladies." A compliment to the stag, all this, probably, but rather heavy odds against him. In spite of this, however, it took the hunters nearly an hour to catch him—at Sowerby Bridge.

Two hours rest they awarded the gallant stag, and then turned him out again to resume the inglorious chase. Right to Ripponden he led them, to be captured there an hour later. After this he had a few days' rest, when he was turned out at Northowram for further sport. For three hours he eluded capture, in the course of his run " falling over a precipice into a stone quarry several yards in perpendicular drop." From this he extricated himself, to be seized finally in a farmyard by a bull-terrier. On these hunts the dogs were harriers, not stag-hounds.

Of the stag's fate or misfortunes after this we are not told; but apparently all was not plain hunting for his guardian, Mr. Moore. When he was hunting with the hounds later near Elland he had to ford the Calder, and his horse sank into deep water and unseated him. Rescuers, it appears, came on the scene only just in time, when " the spark of life was almost extinguished."

There was a sensational meeting of the hounds at the May Pole at Warley, when the dogs broke bounds and rushed into a cottage where the day's baking was spread appetisingly before the hearth. Within minutes the hungry dogs had consumed the lot—loaves, cakes and pastries. The distracted housewife was compensated, we learn, and with a blast on the horn the huntsmen, with their now-satisfied pack, set off for Norland.

Glimpse of a local Bank "Panic."

HALIFAX banks did not escape stormy situations in their early years, but in the main they weathered the "runs." Their most troublous time was in December, 1825, and early 1826, when about 100 London and provincial private banks (many of them northern) suspended payment. The urge to withdraw their money spread to local bank depositors, who became "rude and demanding" as efforts to assuage the rush were made. Nothing but payment in gold would satisfy: Bank of England notes were treated with contempt!

The banks of Rawson and Co., and Rawdon, Briggs and Sons here were both strong, but they suffered a run like the rest—simultaneously with banks in neighbouring towns, one of which had to shut its doors after an hour and a half. For several days with varying pressure the run continued. From the first the banks named paid all who came with "quick dispatch." Mr. H. Ling Roth, who left us the story of local early banking, observes that another bank "took time over it," to conserve resources, and closed at the usual time, leaving a great crowd at the door! Some kept open until a late hour. On the second day, Saturday, the run continued at all the banks; on the Monday it went on all day with unabated fury, but it dwindled at Rawson's bank at 2 p.m. on the Tuesday. By this time, while the banks were trying to hold out against customers' demands for their credit, Mr. Stansfeld Rawson was speeding to the rescue on the road from London. Early in the turmoil he had dashed off in his chaise from the White Lion in Silver Street to draw in London the precious gold sovereigns that could save the situation at the home bank if they could reach it in time.

It was an unparalleled feat. Three days only it took him to accomplish the double journey, escaping the prevalent dangers of the road—accident and robbery. When he arrived at his bank with the gold (£50,000 was the amount Miss Lister, of Shibden Hall, quoted after visiting the Rawson home at this time, but Mr. Ling Roth prefers his estimate of £15,000, based on the weight of gold the chaise could carry) he found a crowd of "withdrawers" still assembled.

Whether the money was used for them is not indicated, but other banks struggling in vain to stem the rush were helped generously from his new supply of sovereigns, and the local panic was gradually stemmed by the knowledge that ample gold was available, and deposits were eventually restored.

Rawsons' bank was for many years in the former Royds' mansion in George Street, part of which is now Somerset House.

A local lock-up of the 19th century.

LONG surviving the Halifax Gaol and Debtors' Prison, were a few local lock-ups in which offenders were secured before being taken before the magistrates. They were used for those whose misdeeds were more serious than offences merely warranting a spell in the stocks. The stocks were usually near the lock-up : it was possible for the Constable to dispose of misbehaving citizens speedily, and, as the solitary local guardian of the law, he was much too busy to take all lawbreakers into custody and to conduct them to the police station to be charged. He had his own temporary remedy.

One such corner where summary justice was dispensed was on the roadside at Illingworth, where, in 1823, a single-storey stone prison was erected, containing four cells. Here, in a very primitive confined space, persons committing serious offences were locked up; and it is recorded that the Constable, who lived conveniently close by, had the duty of bringing from his home a small iron bedstead for a prisoner to use if he was brought in at night. The " case " would then be heard in Halifax at the first opportunity. This prison building is there to-day, next to the well-known stocks outside the churchyard wall—stocks which have been there nearly 260 years, and which could accommodate two unruly occupants together, to the entertainment of the population of Illingworth, who could abuse the victims freely, and to the diversion of passing coach travellers. Since the lock-up ceased to be used as such after about 40 years, the building has been altered to suit its various users, and another storey has been added. But the barred windows, a fan-shaped one over the door and two round windows higher up (all too high for the unhappy occupant to look from) are still in place. The bolt-studded door was backed by a sheet of iron, and the little prison would surely withstand the most violent assault that could be expected from within or without.

Whether or not the ingoing prisoner would have the opportunity to read and digest the earnest, sobering words on the tablet above the the door, every passer-by who could read could take warning from them. It may be supposed that any person who had spent a night in a tiny stone cell there would be unable to resist a glance at the door with its surmounting tablet when afterwards he passed the building; but it could also be possible that as few who passed 100 years ago would read it as do so to-day. "Let him that stole steal no more, but rather Let him labour, working with his hands The thing which is good, that he may have To give to him that needeth." The rest is there for you to read the next time you pass.

The Beadle and the Pinder of Elland.

IN the familiar square building at the corner of the five-road crossing in Elland facing the Town Hall, once lived the Parish Beadle, who was also the Town Pinder. For besides being the " lock-up " in which wrongdoers caught by the Constable were imprisoned temporarily, this building, erected in 1821, was partially a dwelling. For a period it was the lot of the holder of the office of Pinder—then an appointment of the Court Leet of the Duchy of Lancaster—to occupy the domestic portion of the little prison house.

The impounding of wandering animals was an important duty in the days when the highways were mostly narrow lanes, and animals, less enclosed than to-day, strayed more freely; and the Pinder's authority was indisputable. There was an occasion in Elland, however, we are told, when the Pinder's efforts to impound a cow and her calf in the Ainleys pinfold were thwarted very neatly by the animals themselves.

The farmer's wife saw the cow and the calf belonging to her husband passing up the hill in the possession of the Pinder, who was driving them into the enclosure before she could overtake them. But while the man was unlocking the pinfold gate, sternly intent on securing these straying beasts, she called out the pet name she had for the calf. The animal heard her voice and ran off to meet her. The cow instantly followed, and the angry Pinder was outpaced down the hill. By the time he reached the farm both animals were under lock and key in the mistal. He demanded them in vain, and his threats to knock the door down to get them were met with a counter threat of a warrant against him if he touched it. High dispute ensued, but the episode ended in the kitchen, where the wife appeased the Pinder for his loss of dignity by a jug of ale and a round of toasted oatcake!

As the Beadle, the same individual was perhaps more important still, and he was a decorative figure in his blue coat and waistcoat faced with scarlet trimming, his red plush knee breeches and his cocked hat. The stick of office he carried added meaning to his importance. One of his special duties was a Sunday one, for this long white stick went to church with him. In full official uniform he had to walk the aisles, to overawe the disorderly and to give judicious pokes with his stick at those who fell asleep. To dogs that strayed into church, and to evildoers of tender years anywhere, the Beadle was a personage to be feared. " Whoso Keepeth The Law Is Wise," the front wall tablet on his dwelling counselled the people of Elland, as it does to-day.

109

... So they joined the Forces.

AT the beginning of the nineteenth century trade locally became paralysed. As Napoleon overran the Continent, he sought to bring England to her knees by ruining her growing trade with Europe—burning by decree all goods of British manufacture wherever found. Necessities of life were at famine prices. Potatoes rose to 18s. per stone in Halifax; tea was sold by the ounce (at 8d.) owing to scarcity; oatmeal, flour and other commodities were similarly scare and dear.

A subscription fund was opened to provide work to alleviate distress, and for a period about 800 men assembled daily near the markets and were marched up to Highroad Well Moor to prepare the ground for produce and crop-growing, receiving 10d. a day for their work. This came to nothing, for the initial work was not followed up.

So, under these depressed conditions, the army recruiting sergeants met with much success, their processions of soldiers headed by military bands collecting recruits as they perambulated the town with colours flying. A recruit was awarded a bounty of sixteen guineas if he joined "for life," or ten guineas if he signed for seven years. The 33rd Regiment's ("The Havercake Lads") recruiting sergeant had a hard oatcake on the point of his sword on these parades.

In the public-houses, shillings were slipped into tankards of ale to induce young waverers to swear they would serve His Majesty King George III, and coveted, needed shillings were slipped into hands or pockets as tempting bribes—the bounties to follow. There was balloting for the local Militia of 1,100 men, the Volunteers being disbanded, and enlistment secured a ten-pound bounty. The Militia paraded and drilled at the Piece Hall and on Ovenden Moor. Their drum-major became a fascinating sight, flourishing his silver-cupped stick before his ten fifers, twelve drummers, two buglemen and the cymbals, when Colonel Horton, of Howroyd, the commander, had the men on parade.

Great efforts also were made to attract recruits for the Royal Navy by impressing on young men what prizes were to be obtained by privateering. Many ran away to join the men-of-war—some to serve under Nelson at the Battle of Trafalgar, as ten years later many local men were with Wellington's army at Waterloo.

The former Saddle Hotel was a popular recruiting rendezvous. There the resident recruiting officer wore his full-dress long blue coat, buckskin breeches, cocked hat, a nine-inch broad belt carried over one shoulder and jackboots. He, however, apparently selected a different vocation for his own future; for we learn that he became a porter at Alnwick Castle for the Duke of Northumberland.

The Spice of Life.

MANY happenings reveal Halifax's past as anything but dull. There were murders as dramatic as could be imagined. A man walking on the old stone North Bridge in 1819 for instance, was flung over the battlements by an unknown assassin; the incident resulted in pallisades being provided to prevent such atrocities. Two men of Southowram threw a fellow-worker from a window in a Cross Hills mill in 1849, and were sentenced at York Assizes to transportation for 18 years. The planned murder of William Deighton, the Excise Officer, in Savile Road, 1769, was a " national incident " with wide results, and two men eventually hung in chains on Beacon Hill after execution in York, as a gruesome warning. There were others, but we will abandon them for more pleasant happenings after recalling the pickpocket who robbed a gentleman in court of seven guineas during the trial of two murderers of a Scots trader in Halifax in 1782.

The man who sold his wife at The Cross here in 1822 was not unique as a wife-seller. The purchaser was nearly 90, but he had reasons for buying the lady—three children from his marriage with her seven years previously. Unluckily for him the woman's husband, supposed long since dead, returned from the army in foreign parts and claimed her. Negotiations decided that the octogenarian could retain her only if he bought her. The husband led her to The Cross with a halter round her neck, and the deal was struck before many witnesses. We are not told the price of this wife, but another had been sold shortly before for five guineas to " a gentleman who well knew her merit."

Two men of Midgley strike a cheerful picture in 1783, when " after a good supper they ate 10 quarts of water-porridge, made very thick." The wager allowed them 10 minutes, but they did it in eight. A carter who had refreshed himself too well, seeing the stocks at Illingworth, demanded to be put in them; and as he became so unruly at being unheeded, they put him in. Discovering where he was when sobered, he demanded release and redress so abusively that they kept him there.

An enterprising shopkeeper in 1808 advertised his stock of " Portable Pocket Gaslighters," which suggests our modern lighters are not so original as we thought. And, for further variety, a letter to the " Guardian " Editor from Crib Lane 100 years ago, complaining that the cleaners clearly preferred cleaning the " more respectable parts of the town," leaving his locality three inches deep in sludge. This was slyly significant at the time : there had been 70 applicants for a new corps of 16 cleaners, and the latters' unfamiliar efforts came in for much critical comment.

The ups and downs of Stoodley Pike.

THE lonely Pike high on Langfield Moor had more than its share of incident and misfortune, in keeping with the stormy causes of its erection 140 years ago. For unexpected things happened during the first half-century of its vigil 1,300 feet up near the Yorkshire and Lancashire border. Fears of invasion by Napoleon's forces, the suffering and bloodshed promoted by that disturber of the peace of Europe, had aroused strong patriotism in our neighbouring towns and villages, and had prompted Halifax to raise three Corps of Volunteers. When Napoleon had at last been brought to his knees the population rejoiced, and in the Calder Valley they gave expression to their gratitude for peace by subscribing for the erection of a monument high on the moors that would tell its story to succeeding generations.

The foundation stone of the 112ft. monument was laid in the summer of 1814, with wide-shared honours—and with hopes that were high, but misplaced. For Napoleon escaped from Elba early in 1815, before the monument was completed, and the peace was shattered by the resumption of hostilities. The Battle of Waterloo, four months later, terminating Napoleon's career and resulting in the restoration of peace, allowed the erection of the tall tapering pillar, on the square base already built, to proceed. On this massive pedestal—inside which began the staircase of 150 steps, at the top being a small room with a fireplace—was placed the inscription declaring the erection to be a peace monument to commemorate the surrender of Paris to the Allies after the Battle of Waterloo in 1815.

But peace for the monument lasted only forty years. It crashed to the ground on February 8, 1854, on the very day, reports tells us, on which the Russian Ambassador left London before the declaration of war with Russia. An ominous coincidence! And down it remained until, with the restoration of peace in 1856, people of the Calder Valley and the wider district collected £600 for the rebuilding of the monument on an equally prominent site further back on the moor, to the design of a Todmorden architect. The cost was more than £800, but a willing benefactor readily donated the balance.

The " new " Stoodley Pike is a strong sentinel on its lofty eminence while others wars have waged and new invasions threatened. It has not escaped the ravages of long exposure—£150 was spent on repairs in 1889, and a lightning conductor was provided for the monument's protection.

The changing face of Ward's End.

THE large colourful roundabout and the small flower-beds that give such a bright aspect to the Ward's End entrance to Halifax to-day follow many innovations in this open space during the past 150 years. Features for which this " town's end " was the selected site vanished under necessity time and time again as differing problems arose with the changing times.

From old Barum Top at the beginning of the 19th century a lane known as Doctor Lane led down to the open space—very wide open then—and let into its garden walls where it emerged were at least ten water troughs. For water was readily " on tap " here, and horse drinking troughs were a common necessity. The water to feed the 500-gallon tank in the Old Cock Yard (then one of the few reserves of the town's water supply) came under this lane on its way from Well Head; and a water tank for use in case of fire stood also at Ward's End. In later years, to cater for the increasing horse traffic entering and leaving the town, a large square drinking trough was erected near the centre of the open space. The stone troughs in the lane had to be demolished as they became outmoded and as building extension progressed, but their perpetuation in name during nearby development later recalls their former prominence. The square drinking trough gave place to a more substantial eight-sided trough made from local stone that was in use for a long period.

And then, in 1884, a drinking fountain provided by a Halifax woman, Mrs. Leigh, in memory of her mother, Mrs. Prescott, replaced this stone trough at Ward's End. By this time the lane from Barum had become transformed into an important thoroughfare—appropriately renamed Fountain Street. The new fountain was a dominating feature at the five-roads junction. It was described as a " fine, handsome and imposing ornamental structure . . . for the use of the people and for the refreshment of the dumb animals." Erected in polished grey granite, brought from Cornish quarries, it had four taps for the public use, two 100 gallon troughs for horses and four small drinking troughs for sheep and dogs. Its octagonal column relieved by four granite pillars was surmounted by a lamp standard and globe.

The Prescott Fountain remained there for only 14 years; for the electric tramways came to Ward's End, and the open space had to be free of obstructions. Like the Prince Albert Statue the fountain left for another resting place—at King Cross. Now it stands at the top of Savile Park. And Ward's End traffic problems half a century later are solved by a new obstruction—the roundabout. What further changes has the future in store for this " open space?"

The first trip to Blackpool.

OF the 9,000 people in Halifax a century and a half ago most only left the town when their journey could be made on horseback or on foot. Coach travel was for the comparative few. If you were numbered among the gentry, of course, you would journey at your pleasure in your private coach or other equippage. Several handsome vehicles Halifax did boast in 1800; and there were affluent visitors who stayed, in passing through the town, at the inns which were provided with stabling and stage horses for changing for the road. In the Union Cross Inn Yard, for instance, were coach horses in the first-floor stalls, approached by a sloping ramp; and the Old Cock Inn had stabling for fifty horses at one period of its history.

There was no vogue for the short " week-end " habit. A destination on the coast was a long way off in time : you were well into the second day before you saw the sea. But there were enterprising coach people here then, as to-day, and they were beginning to cater for the folk who had sufficient ambition to want to travel to the seaside.

If you were one of these and went to the Upper George Inn early on a Monday morning you might get a seat outside the coach—or an inside seat if you liked your comfort and were clever at arranging things—that would take you to Blackpool. It would not set you down there until Tuesday afternoon, but you would not complain; for this was a splendid innovation in travel—a special coach for Blackpool, for 25s. each way ! If you had still been here in 1809 you could have reserved your seat in advance in a brand new coach, " The Royal Trafalgar," on one of its daily journeys to Manchester, and have taken another coach there for Blackpool. But if you were not at the Rose and Crown Inn before 5 a.m. you would miss this coach, a special fast luxury conveyance carrying only four passengers, for it had to be off to catch that connection before noon.

A more respectable time to go Manchester was mid-day, from the Talbot Inn, where the " Defiance " from Leeds called daily; but Leeds often found its quota of passengers, leaving Halifax would-be travellers standing. (How history still repeats itself !). Perhaps there was not so much glamour in coach travelling in " the good old days " as is so temptingly depicted for us, but might it not have been a happier fate to be left standing at (or in) the old Talbot by the " Defiance " in 1809 than to be left standing in the Manchester queue in 1955, or even in the bus when Bradford does to us what Leeds did to our forbears?

Nights at the old Theatre Royal.

PLAYERS at the old Theatre Royal, Halifax, where many famous actors and actresses appeared during its long existence, had not to be particular about audiences' reception of their efforts, nor had they to be upset by unexpected happenings. Visiting Hamlets, for instance, the first time they picked up the skull thrown from the opened ground by the gravedigger, and declaimed that " he hath borne me upon his back a thousand times," probably were unaware that this skull was the head-piece of a murderer who had hung in chains on Beacon Hill! But they had to put up with this, for it was theatre " property " for several years.

In the early days of this 1789 theatre, " Othello " was being per-formed on a special night, the pit and gallery being crowded and the rows of small boxes that faced the stage " filled with the beauty and fashion of the day." For reasons most incompletely explained for us, the play suddenly closed down on the night's performance as the audience could not recover from its ill-timed mirth.

Apparently some spirited companions of Othello who had spent much time with him in a tavern during the day had secretly altered the backcloth scenery for the bed-chamber episode. When Othello, innocent of the trickery, entered and began his dramatic declamations, the aud-ience roared with unrestrained laughter. All Desdemona and Othello could do was to gaze round in astonishment " to know the cause." And the play closed on that unfinished scene.

The gallery of the Royal was extended over the Shakespear Tavern, as the hostelry round the corner was then styled. This inn was very popular with the theatregoers of the day, and there was a way through to its bar and comforts directly from the theatre. During the playing season of three months, when performances were given three nights a week, the Shakespeare was open until the small hours. Here the elite who were without carriages would wait for Sedan chairs to take them home, and the revellers could continue their entertainment at will. Friday night was the fashionable night of the week, and programmes were printed on white satin, lettered in gold, so that ladies would not soil their white silk gloves.

When, in 1826, a stud of trained horses appeared in " The Battle of Waterloo," it was declared to be " a marvel how it was managed " on the very small stage. The old theatre, with its contrasts of elegance and crudity, was very much a part of the town; the Halifax Cricket Club, short of money in 1840 and 1841, was given Shakespearean benefit nights, and pink silk programmes heralded a " benefit " performance for the Infirmary in 1855.

"Scenes" in the old theatres.

A VISIT to the Halifax Theatre in the early 1800's could be depended on to provide plenty of sensation. But however exciting the melodrama of the players, there was often more excitement and drama among the audience. Rowdyism and horseplay reached such a pitch that it became difficult for any production to obtain an audience of the more orderly townspeople. Nightly the shows were being ruined by the " rowdies " in the cheaper parts, and the theatre was reduced to a very unhappy state in its chequered history. The harassed manager brought about a very sudden change, however, at the end of 1832, and readers of the new " Guardian " were soon reading : " We are gratified to find that the manager has made a vigorous and successful effort to repress the disorderly conduct in the gallery." The manager's method with the destroyers of his theatre's reputation was as simple as it was ingenious. He announced in the play-bills that the constables had been ordered to be on the lookout for those unruly persons who were disturbers of the peace, and that any other person in the audience who gave information to them of such offenders would receive as a reward a free ticket for a whole season of performances. The effect was immediate—the improvement being prompted either by fear of the constables or of the theatre full of potential informers. We learn from the paper that " the inhabitants of the upper regions have since been perfectly quiet and decorous, and the public may enjoy now without annoyance the exertions of the best provincial companies." The manager's stroke proved excellent publicity also, and the theatre benefited doubly.

One dramatic night at a temporary theatre at the Fairground, the audience was assembling to see a sensational performance entitled " Red Dick, The Tiger of California." This was forty years later, but the new decorum of Halifax Theatre had not reached the Fairground shows. There was a battle in the gallery before the play began, and this caused a great rush of people towards the centre away from the fray.

At the end of the first act a cry was raised that the gallery was giving way, but somehow these fears were quieted. In the middle of the second act, however, the whole gallery went down with a crash, carrying with it the hundreds of people crowded on it. There was complete panic, and many people suffered injuries and shock. But this catastrophe resulted in more strict control by regulations governing the safety of audiences.

" Laughing-stock " punishments.

HALIFAX inflicted drastic, and often undignified penalties for wrongdoing right up to the early 19th century, when the most trivial
misdemeanours could offend against the law.   Indignity in punishment
was deliberate : the victim in the pillory, the whipping-post, the ducking
stool or the stocks would be the more readily reformed by a penalty that
permitted his fellow-citizens to contribute to his punishment as an entertainment for themselves.   And the public made the most of these enlivening occasions.

There was a pillory at the junction of Old Market with Northgate
up to 1786.   It was a wooden contraption, with holes in a crosspiece for
the offender's neck and arms, and in it he stood upright to endure his
punishment for varying periods.   Its declared use was for " the better
exposure of cheats, imposters, libellers, immoral people and political
offenders to open shame, derision and practical abuse in the form of
filth and foul things being hurled at them."   Thus were the victim-
baiters invited to contribute any torment they could invent.

Women were not subjected to the pillory.   The devisers of punish-
ments had something equally unpleasant, if more speedy, for misbehaving
females, which again invited public derision and amusement.   Halifax,
Sowerby Bridge, Elland and Stainland each had their ducking-stool.   The
wrongdoers, the " noisy ones and drunks," referred to in accounts of
those days as " alewives," were placed in a stool or chair suspended over
a pond or river from a long pole mounted on a pivot.   When the other
end of the pole was raised by those administering the punishment, down
went the helpless offender into the water, to be completely immersed the
prescribed number of times, and to come up again presumably cured of
any desire to offend again.   This penalty was inflicted on the wayward
women of Elland, for instance, from the end of the old bridge over
the river.

We had our whipping post, and an occasional barbarous practice
of flogging at the tail of a cart drawn through the streets, for certain
offences.   Both men and women were liable to this whipping " remedy."
There were the lock-ups too, for impounding persons to be charged.   The
peaceful-looking stocks near Halifax Parish Church, at Illingworth, at
Southowram, and elsewhere, are relics of a not-so-amusing punishment
for their victims, as everybody knows.   Oldest of all was the gibbet,
which has received much publicity as a feature of old Halifax.

The coachman jumped over North Bridge.

THE diligence from Kendal was passing through Halifax at Christmas in 1781 on its three days' routine journey to London. After a brief stop here the coach resumed its journey very early on Christmas Eve, while it was still quite dark.

John Davy's spirited four-horse team was on the new six-arch stone bridge that would carry them over the Hebble almost before they had got into their stride. And when they were on the bridge it happened. The driver never reached the toll bar at the north end of the bridge . . .

Quoting the newspaper report: " . . . his horses running restive, jammed the carriage close to the battlements thereon, when being under the necessity of leaving his box to apply the whip as a remedy for their stupidity, and being a total stranger to his situation he jumped out over the bridge; by which one of his legs was broken, and he was so terribly bruised that he languished till Tuesday and then expired."

The fatality that overtook poor John Davy in Halifax was surely unique. Yet it could happen as easily as it can be imagined, in the pitch darkness of winter, when the luckless driver was unaware that his horses were standing on a bridge.

Two Halifax women had an unenviable coach journey experience about this time. Their coach, from the White Horse, reached London safely, and so did they. But their luggage, which had been sent on earlier by the Blue Fly stage wagon, did not. The trunks were found some time afterwards in the Pontefract region—rifled, filled with earth, and flung into a pond. Here was a problem for the two women: to be in the London of 1782 without possessions and three days' communication distance from home. The missing property was not recovered, we are told. It seems that the Blue Fly driver looked in at a certain place to have his fill of gin, and while there the plan was concocted which resulted in our innocent townswomen being robbed of their possessions.

But our local stage coach travellers could be romantically true to the Christmas cards and the stories. In proof just let us recall the fortunate young lady from Halifax whose coach, before reaching the outskirts of London, was held up by a highwayman. For good reasons there were two " mentions " of this young woman's adventure in the Leeds paper which reported our local news in those times. The bravery and gallantry displayed by a gentleman travelling in the coach during the lively encounter with the highwayman led to a friendship which resulted, after a discreet interval, in the second reference—a notice of marriage.

The Piece Hall opening.

THE Manufacturers' Hall was finished—after four and a half years of negotiations, meetings, balloting as to site, tendering, building. Halifax had its "exchange," where the spun wool and the woven pieces could be traded. Interest in the immense, unique structure was widespread. To the scattered spinners with their wheels, and to the hand-loom weavers whose produce had to be brought from far and wide over the pack-horse routes, the Piece Hall was the new "Mecca" where the merchants and clothiers would be found. No longer was it necessary for their goods to be sold in the inns or in the streets. The "clothiers," as both buyers and sellers were called then, could rent one of the 315 rooms in "The Rustic," or "The Arcade," or "The Collonade," of the three-storey edifice. They could leave their horses at their favourite inns, go to the Hall to transact their business and adjourn to the inns for refreshment and the company of friends.

On January 2, 1779—probably the most important day in Halifax's commercial history—the Piece Hall was to be opened for business; the day before was devoted to celebrating the event, being New Year's Day and a customary holiday. The Hall was thrown open to the population. A grand fireworks display was to round off the day's happenings. First there was the assembly in the great open space of the Piece Hall of people engaged in the various trades of the town, and of visiting gentlemen with their ladies for whom seats had been prepared. It was a picturesque scene, the men in their coloured coats and breeches, three-cornered hats and wigs, hose and buckled shoes; and ladies in their bonnets and muffs, and, on this occasion, their finery cloaked against the wintry weather. The new Piece Hall had a wonderful send-off. Headed by bands of music the procession left the Hall and paraded the town—which did not extend far above Barum Top or beyond Ward's End. The Christmas evergreens were still displayed, banners were unfurled, and many timbered houses had been given new paint.

After dark the fireworks of "the great Signor Petro, the Italian pyrotechnist," illuminated the Hall with set pieces and coloured fire—a display of which the people of Halifax were a part. And the next morning the bell in the little turret over the West Gate, with its golden fleece weathercock rang at 10 a.m., to signal the opening of the ponderous north door with a silver key for the first day's business.

Salterhebble Docks.

IN the latter half of the eighteenth century, much activity centred upon Salterhebble, and this increased as the schemes to complete the Calder and Hebble Navigation system developed. In 1768 a meeting of tradesmen and gentry at the old Talbot Inn in Woolshops had resulted in the great engineer, John Smeaton, who had recently completed the third Eddystone Lighthouse, being engaged to plan canal and river navigation to connect the Calder wharves at Wakefield with the Hebble. Later, the section to Salterhebble was included, and this canal, with the extensions to Sowerby Bridge and to Rochdale that followed, played a great part in the industrial importance of Halifax and the whole North of England, for the two coasts were thus linked—via Salterhebble.

Transport of Yorkshire and Lancashire produce had previously been possible only by pack-horse and wagon, on the long tracks and hill-top routes. But the canals changed all this. It was estimated that a barge drawn by a single horse could move the load of 600 pack-horses; and much heavier goods, such as timber, stone and coal could be carried easily and cheaply.

Floods, frost and fire provided many setbacks. In 1768 a great flood washed away much of the new work on the Salterhebble to Sowerby Bridge section, and a year's delay was caused. An improved scheme was planned, and 1770 saw this section opened. The extension to Rochdale was completed in 1798. The Halifax civil engineer, Thomas Bradley, designed the branch canal from Bailey Hall which was joined up to the busy docks in 1828. By this time there was a weekly service to London, others linking with the Mersey, Humber and Trent. The aqueduct at Salterhebble was burst by a flood in 1828, but the repaired waterway was reopened after only three weeks. Fire destroyed the wharf warehouse in 1832. In January, 1861, the Brighouse-Elland-Sowerby Bridge sections of the canal were frozen so solidly that 27 horses—some walking on the ice—were employed to pull an " ice-boat," and it took two days to clear the route. Behind the ice breaker were nine barges laden with much-needed coal for the mills.

Then the railways began to threaten the country's 4,000 miles of canals. Our engineer, Bradley, was not alarmed, however. In a warning report to the worried navigation authorities he pointed out the impossibility of railways superseding canals as a means of transport : their cost, danger and difficulties in our hilly country ensured this. A speed of eight to twelve miles an hour would satisfy any reasonable tradesmen, he said; the "aquatic medium" would maintain its superiority, and the inland waterways' existence was a certainty " to the latest period of time." What would he say if he saw the Salterhebble Docks in the middle of the twentieth century?

A King came for a night.

WHEN riders brought the news into Halifax on that afternoon in 1768, the townspeople who were at the moment in those narrow streets, Back Lane and Loveledge Lane (later to become Cheapside and George Street), must have experienced an unusual sense of anticipation. For a unique Royal procession was approaching. And the pageantry that soon invaded Halifax was surely more stately and colourful than any the spectators had seen or had expected.

Outriders in Royal livery headed the cavalcade bringing King Christian VII of Denmark, who was travelling as Prince George, to break his journey here for the night. Fifty horses had been provided in Leeds for the stage of the journey to Halifax—for the six coaches that had four horses each, for the post-chaises and the attendants and outriders. The arrival with his retinue of the young King, wearing silver-trimmed blue uniform, can only be imagined now, as may the evening's social occasion prepared by his host, Mr. John Royds, in his house with its beautiful salon.

At the time of this Royal visit this town mansion (part of which is now Somerset House) was at the extreme edge of Halifax, its forecourt and gardens covering much of the ground now traversed by Powell Street and Rawson Street. It had been erected only two years previously, and it was to be the scene of many notable events and visits during its early history.

The Danish King was engaged on a leisurely tour of England, mainly in the North, and as it was conducted on the lavish scale of which its passage through Halifax was an indication, this was no light achievement. Christian VII was 19 years old. At 17 he had married the English Princess Caroline Mathilde, 15 year-old sister of the reigning King George III. She did not accompany him on this eccentric tour, and, indeed, history records that he refused to allow his young Queen to revisit her native country. The King's companion was a young fascinating North German doctor he had met on his travels—who, incidentally, shortly after their return became the Queen's lover and the virtual ruler of Denmark for a period, until he was arrested and executed, and the Queen banished from the country.

More than 600 miles were covered by the Royal tourists, and ducal houses in the South entertained him as his tour became extended. From Halifax the King's route lay towards The Bull's Head in Manchester, where he was to lodge the next night, and it fell to our many inn stables the following morning to provide the 50 horses for the stage of the procession's progress over the rough roads of the Pennines.

The Bath Parade.

HALIFAX can go down in history as having possessed up-to-date and even luxurious open-air bathing facilities—200 years ago. The Baths, originally serving a town population of under 7,000, appear to have lacked little in the way of amenities, and there must have been, too, a salubrity about the atmosphere down by the Hebble Brook in those days, for the fashionable Bath Parade was there, by the water side.

Brief sections of Bath Lane and Lilly Lane, which led down towards the Baths from Church Street, remain to-day, but most of the old property between the Parish Church and Shaw Syke disappeared when the site for the railway and the goods yards was developed more than a century ago. It is not easy to imagine the surroundings and the setting of the Baths 100 years before that, with the present Waterside in mind, but the surprising picture deserves to be recalled.

The Baths buildings were of plain red brick, but they were constructed on an elaborate scale. There was an imposing row of arches along one side of the oblong pool, bordering a wide sidewalk that would do credit to a modern open-air bathing pool. On the other sides were tastefully arranged shrubberies, giving the Baths a secluded setting; and, presumably, the sun would occasionally warm the ample space for lounging after bathing. There was also a " large lawn for the exercise of the manly games of bowls and quoits." Besides the swimming bath there were cold and warm shower and vapour baths, and dressing and waiting rooms. The water was supplied from a spring rising near the premises —not from the Hebble. In 1852, when the Baths were already about 100 years old, they were entirely renovated before reopening for the summer on April 30, and a gay occasion—known as " the Bath Feast " —was held, to give the season a good start. The grounds and pleasure gardens, we are told, presented " a highly ornamental and genial appearance," and great attention had been paid in providing for the comfort of the bathers and the gratification of visitors. The Baths, privately owned, were conducted at this period by a Mrs. J. W. Anderson, who was noted for her cheerful and obliging manner with her patrons. For the reopening ceremony, at which there was a large attendance, including " the leading professional and commercial men," a quadrille band had been engaged to enliven the company, and sumptuous refreshments were supplied by Mrs. Anderson.

All of which suggests that this was quite a delectable resort down by the Hebble Brook in Halifax—hardly the kind imagined without a reminder when the old days are given thought.

Smallpox inoculation two centuries ago.

AN intimate picture of a critical time in Halifax emerges from a past century at the Mulcture Hall. Smallpox was carrying away many from the population. The record appears in an autobiography written " for the instruction and amusement of his children and descendants " by Thomas Wright, who was born in the Hall in 1736. At the time the epidemic was raging Thomas was four or five years old : his grandfather, father, mother and a sister had all died—this sister, Martha, " a beautiful little girl," he says, having died from the small pox some time before he himself contracted it. His grandmother alone was left to look after Thomas, and of her he says that " being extremely fond of me as the only remains of her offspring and consequently very anxious to preserve my life she was persuaded by Doctor Nettleton who was very intimate with the family, to let him inoculate me as the safest method against the dread disease." This was in 1740—half a century before vaccination against smallpox was practised, for Jenner was not yet born.

The doctor, we learn from Thomas's account, seated him in the left wing of the Hall, bared his arms, made an incision in each above the bend of the elbow, introduced the serum and bound up the parts. A young man, " the doctor's apprentice," stood by all the time. The doctor gave Thomas a penny when it was over, saying he was a fine boy and the first child upon whom he had operated who had not wept. A week later the fever came : the doctor, his wife and the apprentice were close in attendance and very anxious over the outcome. The practice of inoculation depended for its credit in the neighbourhood upon the success of this and a few other instances. They gave him syrups and sweetmeats. But Thomas reports that " by improper treatment, that of keeping me too hot both without and within, which aftertimes and improved knowledge have rectified, the eruption was great, and I was much hazarded." Although he survived, he suffered an eye defect and was a good deal pitted. The practice of inoculation was brought into disrepute locally, we are told, because several of those inoculated about the same time died.

After he recovered Thomas was sent to school—" first to a petty school and afterwards to a kind of Free School higher up the street than our Hall, on the same side." This was the Blue Coat School, belonging to the Waterhouse Charities, which then stood near the Parish Church.

The bell rang twice a day.

FACING Sowerby's ancient main street stands a neat row of half a dozen small houses which bear two inscriptions on crests worked in stone. The dwellings were built in 1862 on the site of six small single-deck almshouses built early in the eighteenth century which had a story surely unique in its strangeness. On a centre one was a memorial inscription that read : " Behold my mother and my brethren "—an expressive reason for the benefaction.

Under a condition imposed by the benefactor, the three men and three women who occupied the dwellings had to be unmarried, must have been born in the chapelry of Sowerby, had to be sixty or over, and were to remain single so long as they lived there.

This last condition was for the specified reason that the apartments could accommodate no more than one. Each occupant received 2s. 6d. per month under the endowment. The trustees had to be satisfied that these persons were " virtuous and good natured and such as have kept off the parish by their own industry " until age or infirmity made this impossible.

But there was more to it than this. Punctually at 9 a.m. and 3 p.m. daily, one of the occupants rang a bell (except on Sundays, when the second bell rang at five o'clock) as a signal for the twice-daily routine that had to be followed.

The bell summoned the five inhabitants of the other dwellings to that of the one who rang, who had to read to them a chapter of the New Testament and offer a prayer from a book of devotions. For carrying out this compulsory duty the reader received five shillings quarterly, but any of the others omitting to assemble for this reading forfeited a halfpenny each time to the reader, unless a sound reason for absence was presented. The monthly allowance could be seriously reduced or entirely forfeited by neglect to answer the calling bell twice daily !

The little row of one-deckers became dilapidated, and it was de-molished after nearly a century and a half of useful existence, being replaced by the present more commodious dwellings. The old occu-pants, it was said at the opening ceremony, when a substantial tea was provided for them, were highly pleased with their new lofty rooms and the comfortable furnishings. Less restrictive regulations were agreed to and the allowance was increased.

On one of the stone crests may be seen to-day the memorial inscription to Gertrude Elizabeth, only daughter of Mr. John Rawson, of Brockwell, in whose memory he built the houses in 1862; on the other Mr. Rawson perpetuated a reminder that Elkanah Horton built the original almshouses in 1728.

In the Debtor's Gaol.

WE may come very much nearer home than the debtors' prison in which Charles Dickens placed Mr. Pickwick, for in Halifax Gaol there was a section for our townspeople who couldn't or wouldn't pay their debts. Many unruly happenings occurred in this gaol, such as the uproar in 1711, when " prisoners brake the partitions of the Gaole and was soe turbulent " that under orders from the Duke of Leeds who had title of the property, Justices of the Peace came to view the breaches and directed that " stronger fortifications " be erected, at a cost of fifteen pounds.

In earlier days persons had been committed to the prison for three months for debts of 3s. or 4s., and on three occasions a local physician was locked up there. His maximum debt was £2. There was a touch of respectability about the apartments behind the gaoler's house in Gaol Lane which were set apart for debtors who could afford to pay for superior accommodation. In 1706, an arrested debtor had to pay a fee of 2s. to the gaoler, and after 24 hours' custody a gaol fee of 17s. 4d. There were more fees as their stay was extended, including 10s. for the turnkey. The longer they stayed the more difficulty they were finding in paying the debt for which they were locked up, as they could not earn, so their spells in gaol were usually short in consequence. In 1785 new rules for the more stringent government of the prison were approved. Prisoners were split into two classes—" gentlemen " and " yeomen, tradesmen and artisans." A gentleman had to pay 16s. for his fee and his first week's commons at table, a tradesmen 13s. 6d. Nightly for his bed a gentleman paid 4d., a tradesman 2d.; but when the gaoler lodged two or more prisoners in one bed they paid 3d. between them! For swearing or misdemeanour prisoners were fined twelve pence, and if they did not pay this to the gaoler distraint could be made on their goods. They could be placed in irons if suspected of trying to escape.

Debtors were ordered to bed at 9-30—but liquor was allowed until ten o'clock. In the winter of 1830 the prisoners returned thanks to a private donor of £1 and two dozen loads of coal . . . a strange blend of severity and leniency for our forbears who did not pay their debts— which in many cases must have been less than the fees and fines non-payment cost them.

Old Tristram's long vigil.

IT is a pity the effigy of Old Tristram standing there against his pillar in Halifax Parish Church cannot tell us about his two centuries' vigil on behalf of "The Poor," and something of the real Tristram of old he is alleged to resemble. It would be interesting to hear from him whether he really was missing from his post for a time, having been stealthily abducted, carried from the church and robbed of his collection, then left deserted in a lane on the outskirts of the town, as we are vaguely told. His presence to-day must satisfy us that if he did have adventure he was, happily, discovered and was taken back to the church.

But at least there seems no doubt of his having been there as far back as the early seventeen hundreds, when lived John Aked, "Carver of Old Tristram and of the Royal Arms in the Parish Church." For it was in 1704 that John Aked was paid ten pounds and fifteen shillings for "painting the Queen's Arms in part." The Tristram the figure represents, we are told, was educated in the Workhouse; that he became a beggar when he reached manhood and that his son followed his example and became a mendicant. Their names are in the parish books of the 16th century, in Dr. Favour's time. A man named Tristram, said to be a descendant, was buried in Halifax in 1813, and the registers contain the names of several of the same name who were cordwainers in the town. The curious apparel that adorns the carved figure is declared to be representative of a 17th century beggar's costume, and there may be reason enough for his being so dressed in spite of his being a likeness of a 16th century character. He had to be repainted at times, and "repaired," and John Aked's original style of dress for Old Tristram might have changed more than once through the centuries.

One unnamed craftsman who attended to the patriarchal figure with his long hair and flowing beard and heavy moustache is on record, at any rate. He was paid one pound "for repairing and painting Old Tristram, for piecing his nose and making a new underlip, one thumb from the last joint and a pair of upper leathers to his shoes"; for painting his face and combing his beard; for painting a new pair of black breeches and a "new coat of fashionable brown, and white stockings"; and for touching-up the poor box and rewriting on it the petition to feeling hearts: "Pray Remember the Poor," that Old Tristram still presents to all who pass by.

A Five-day cock-fight.

"MANY gentlemen" assembled about the pit in the new cock-fighting house behind the Cross (the Union Cross Hotel) on a certain Monday in 1680. Not every week was such a battle waged in Halifax, even in the heyday of cock-fighting—and the birds did not do all the fighting. The day began with the appointment of judges to match the cocks, and this appears to have been done with such stern authority by some that they were defied and challenged by others, a lively rivalry being promoted at the outset. Extremely biased they all were, however, in favour of the birds of the "gentlemen." For when "the poorer sort" of Halifax brought their cocks, to put them in the pit to fight first, there was a tremendous set-to.

One of the judges, outraged, is quoted as shouting: "What have beggars to do fighting gentlemen?" an offending remark that could not go unchallenged. And it did not. A young man, championing the insulted, tripped the offender up by the heels, and the two fell to blows. Spectators took sides, and the "gentlemen" and the "poorer sort" fought wildly for a long time; whether there was any cock-fighting at all that day is not clear.

Most of Tuesday passed with a similar merry ferocity, until one combatant impatient at the delay in the contests, drew his rapier and swore he would run it through the next that struck another stroke. An inspired threat, this, for instantly the combatants were quieted—and cocks were placed in the pit. For the rest of the week the cock-fighting went on, interspersed as excitement got the better of the cockers and their followers by battles between the rival factions. An abundance of money was lost and won, we learn; and the company drank all night and played at dice and were "so high in swearing and ranting at the Cross that they were heard far into the town."

A popular figure during this event was a certain "Lord E." whom we find on horseback at the inn doorway, calling for sack and inviting onlookers to drink, then riding wildly along the Corn Market flinging invitations to all and sundry, and back to the Cross with the crowd flocking round him.

Many went home with heavy heads and empty purses. One person who was much troubled by all this was Oliver Heywood, who wrote with grieved reproof of one who engaged in the contest, that he "stakt 15 half-crowns at a cast, it's thought he lost 40 pounds. Oh, dreadful!"

On Elland Bridge.

ELLAND BRIDGE has carried three and a half centuries of history. Its two wooden predecessors, the first built in 1579, were destroyed by the flooded river after a few years. The new stone bridge cost only £484 in 1617, we are told, but it had already provided the link with Halifax and the North for 280 years when in 1879 a wagonette brought council officials to reopen it after its widening (the second widening) from 22½ feet to 36 feet. In 1955 it is still rarely without a crossing vehicle.

The bridge shared in a wonderful day for the women of Elland in 1859, when a full dozen of Mr. Lynch's best greys from Halifax pranced across drawing " his most dashing vehicles with servants in livery fine enough for a Lord Mayor's Day procession." For there were four smart weddings that November morning, three at the church and one—the first to be celebrated there—at the Independent Chapel. No wonder the " Guardian " reported that the many sightseers had their tastes gratified and that the church bells rang merrily.

The narrow bridge was a popular feature of Elland. Here one could lean on the parapet and ruminate. One could have seen, the year after those weddings, the eccentric local character lie on the parapet when a pedestrian approached, have heard him shock the passer-by by announcing he was ending his life, and have seen him roll off into the river thirty feet below. But one would know that after floundering in the water as if in danger of drowning, he would contrive to scramble ashore and resume his street hawking, his clothes soaked, and boast of his skill in saving his life. For this habit brought him much notoriety and was good for business.

The bridge's narrow roadway was turned into a race-track one June night in 1845 by two spirited young sparks returning from Halifax Fair in their gigs. They raced their horses across at full speed side by side; the wheels became entangled, the gigs overturned on the bridge, and their owners were picked up unconscious.

From the suspended chair of the ducking-stool set up at the end of the bridge troublesome women of Elland—the " noisy ones and drunks," referred to as " alewives "—were immersed in the chilly Calder the prescribed number of times, to come up resolved presumably, not to offend again !

And can one to-day imagine the hub of activity that centred for a century on those wharves of the busy new canal that passed under the extended bridge from 1758 and joined in making local history?

Sunday in Halifax 300 years ago.

IF we had lived here in 1657 we should have realised that almost any-thing that could happen on a Sunday was forbidden! In that year a Proclamation was read in the Parish Church applying a rigid rule to Halifax. The Puritan Parliament had passed a law "for the better observance of the Sabbath," and two Justices of the Peace had the duty of enforcing this law in the town. Under the Proclamation even "every levity of step or gesture" which could be construed as vanity or profanity was prohibited. Like "absenting himself from Church or Chappell"— declared a profanation of the Lord's Day—it subjected the offender to a fine of ten shillings.

Many harmless practices in which we engage now on Sundays would then have incurred fines and severe reprimands by the justices. We could not have carried burdens or have done any "worldly labours"; as for offering any wares for sale, or buying, travelling or engaging in pastimes —these were unforgivable, and the hand of the law would have pounced on us.

Had we slipped into an alehouse or tavern, or been found "tippling within any house or shop," or dancing or singing profanely, we would be denounced as very evil persons, and those who lodged or entertained us would have been brought before the justices and fined with us.

A telling point about the Proclamation was that the officers of the church in which it was read periodically were to search for, find out and inform against offenders, to apprehend and stop them with or without warrant, on pain for neglect in the performance of this duty they themselves being under severe censure. The Proclamation was addressed to "ye Constables, Churchwardens and Overseers of ye Town of Halifax," concluding with the ominous phrase: "faile not at your perills."

Nearly 150 years later, when strict observance of the Sabbath was again attempted, some of our less sedate ancestors were rounded up and fined. The Sunday relaxation of three gentlemen of Northowram was disturbed: they were fined for "diverting themselves in sports and pastimes and neglecting public worship on the Lord's Day." And some unlucky boys were brought before the Vicar of Halifax for profaning the Sabbath by playing at trap-ball (a form of knur-and-spell) in the fields during the time of Divine service; they were fined and reprimanded.

But we could have escaped these penalties and have behaved much as we liked if we were under 14, because we should have been deemed not to know when we were doing wrong.

Halifax Beacons in four centuries.

A HUNDRED years ago—recently as time goes for our beacons— many Halifax people still held that the beacon should not be lit on any peaceful occasion : it was a signal of danger and it could cause alarm with dire results. But it was too much to expect that those who accompanied the new beacon to the top of Beacon Hill in 1856 could resist lighting the fire in the pan when they had erected it. Four " handsome and powerful grey horses " had drawn the wagon up the hill after parading the streets in a procession headed by the Haley Hill Sax Horn Band. It was midnight when the fire-pan was fixed in position and with due rejoicing the fire was lighted. Places farther afield where it was not known that Halifax was having a new beacon, were roused to temporary alarm—as the cautious had prophesied. When this beacon was alight in 1902, during the modified celebrations of the postponed Coronation of Edward VII, it must have been overshadowed—or " overlit "—by the nearby bonfire that was 17 feet long, 15 wide and 14 high, built up with 115 tons of wood and material, with plenty of coal, and drenched with 60 gallons of oil !

With the predecessor of this beacon, erected in 1745, it was serious business when the fire blazed its warnings; rebellions and risings frequently threatened, and it was ready in the chain of signals when Napoleon's invasion appeared imminent. And the beacon before that, dating from 1615, played a noteworthy part in many alarms. There was the sudden scare during the Revolution in 1688 when this beacon blazed the warning received from Leeds, where an express messenger from York had brought news of the approach of the enemy. This enemy was the lately disbanded Irish and Scots who, it was declared, had burnt many towns, including Birmingham and Northampton, and were coming northward. Later news was given out in Leeds that " Halifax was on fire and Huddersfield was burnt "—an exaggerated alarm, fortunately. It gave " call-to-arms " signals, as tests of the speed with which the town could prepare to defend itself.

Another hundred years back there was the beacon in the chain of fires that could flash warnings from Land's End to John o' Groats, and which was held in readiness when the Spanish Armada was expected in English waters. The preparedness of this Halifax beacon was the command of the first Queen Elizabeth : and now, four centuries later, a beacon burned on this same historic spot to celebrate the Coronation of her namesake.

Contents.

CONTENTS (continued)—

CONTENTS (continued)— Page